THE SECOND WORLD WAR IN PHOTOGRAPHS

1942

JOHN CHRISTOPHER & CAMPBELL McCUTCHEON

AMBERLEY

First published 2015

Amberley Publishing
The Hill, Stroud
Gloucestershire, GL5 4EP

www.amberley-books.com

British Library Cataloguing in Publication Data.
A catalogue record for this book is available from the British Library.

ISBN 978 1 4456 2211 8 (print)
ISBN 978 1 4456 2227 9 (ebook)

Typeset in 11pt on 15pt Sabon.
Typesetting and Origination by Amberley Publishing.
Printed in the UK.

Contents

An image from the battlefront in Tunisia. Sergeant Richard Sumner who, reportedly, single-handedly captured a machine-gun nest. He is shown here holding a trophy of his exploits, a German MG34 machine gun.

Introduction

1942 began with the completion of Japanese invasions in South East Asia and would end with the successful Allied invasions of North Africa. The year also began with disasters on all fronts for the Allies and ended with a war whose tide had definitely turned, with success on all fronts and a gradual but convincing build-up to a return to northern Europe.

On 1 January 1942, at the Arcadia Conference in Washington, twenty-six Allied countries agree to follow the Atlantic Charter principles and sign the United Nations Declaration. The agreement is to direct their 'full resources' against Germany, Italy and Japan and to not agree to separate peace treaties or agreements with any one while the others still fight. This United Nations Declaration is the beginning of the founding of the post-war United Nations organisation. In the Philippines, US General Douglas MacArthur uses both US and Filipino troops to defend Bataan and the island of Corregidor. Manila, the Filipino capital, has already fallen. Around 80,000 troops will resist the Japanese until the Philippines finally fall in a few months. General Sir Archibald Wavell takes charge of a new American, British, Dutch and Australian command on 3 January and Chinese nationalist leader Chiang Kai-shek takes over as commander of troops in China.

In Russia, Joseph Stalin orders a general offensive on all fronts on 5 January. Initial success sees the Russians capture German transport, food, ammunition and weapons. Soon, the Germans are holding their own and using new defensive tactics to contain the Russian attacks. British, Indian and Australian troops are retreating from Malaya towards Singapore. The Japanese land in the north-east of the peninsula and are rapidly heading south. Kuala Lumpur falls on 12 January. Between 9 and 21 January, the battle of the Valdai Hills is fought in the Moscow sector. The Russians recapture nine towns between Smolensk and Lake Ilmen as they penetrate 75 miles into German-held territory. 10 January sees the invasion by Japanese forces under General Tomoyuki Takahashi of the Dutch East Indies. Oil-rich, they are an important part in the Japanese plans to conquer South East Asia. Celebes is attacked, as is Amboina. Bali, Timor and East Java soon fall. Borneo is attacked from Tarakan, and Japanese forces move from Indochina to take Sumatra and Java. Rommel agrees on 12 January to a plan by his officers to counter-attack the British and Australians in the desert. The Allies in the desert are weakened as the Germans and Italians have regained a modicum of control over the Mediterranean, and the Australians have shipped two divisions to the Far East along with the 7th Armoured Brigade. The campaign in Burma kicks off on 12 January with an invasion from Thailand, and Burmese separatists help the Japanese. The area around Moulmein sees severe battles between Japanese and British, Indian and Burmese troops. Burma has the only viable route into nationalist China and it is important that this route is kept open.

War crimes are on the agenda and on 13 January, the Allies agree to prosecute those Axis leaders and soldiers responsible for war crimes. Off the coast of the United States, Operation Drum Roll begins. This is the code name for U-boat attacks against shipping off the USA. In the first month, U-boats sink twenty vessels. Various factors contribute to the total, including a rather stupid decision by the USA not to insist on blackout conditions along the coast, meaning any ships are silhouetted by the lights of US civilians. In February, the Caribbean is targeted by the U-boats. Field Marshal Reichenau is killed in an aircraft crash on 16 January and is replaced by Field Marshal Bock on 19 January. 5,500 Germans and Italians are captured on 17 January in Libya after Halfaya falls to the Allies. U-boats have extended their reach into the Arctic too on this day, with U-454 sinking HMS *Matabele* and SS *Hamatris*, a merchant vessel from convoy PQ-8, which is carrying valuable war goods to the beleaguered Russians.

The Russians, under Marshal Timoshenko, attack on the Donets River on 18 January in an attempt to trap units from two German armies. Within the week, the advance is halted by the Germans. Perhaps the most sinister event of the Second World War, the 'Final Solution', is agreed at Wannsee, Berlin, by Reinhard Heydrich and other powerful Nazis, including Himmler and Göring. The mass killing of Jews and other undesirables has already been happening in Eastern Europe for many months but the plans enacted at Wannsee will see the industrial killing of a whole race of people. Rabaul, in New Britain, is attacked by aircraft from four Japanese carriers on 20 January, while two Japanese submarines attack Midway, which is located at the far end of the Hawaiian island chain. Australian navy vessels sink a Japanese submarine off Darwin, while attacks are made by the Japanese on Borneo, New Ireland and the Solomons on 23 January, as they continue their expansion in the Pacific.

On 21 January, Rommel begins his second offensive, moving from El Agheila to attack Agedabia. The Eighth Army is caught unawares and is soon pushed back past Benghazi, which falls on 29 January. 440,000 civilians are evacuated from the besieged city of Leningrad, beginning on 22 January; the mass relocation takes fifty days. While many civilians still remain in the city under constant German bombardment, the remainder have left for new homes behind the lines. In the Far East, between 23 and 24 January, American and Filipino forces withdraw further from the Japanese in Bataan, while four US destroyers, aided by Dutch bombers, attack a convoy of Japanese ships in the Makassar Strait. Four of the Japanese troop transports are lost. Thailand declares war on the US and Britain on 25 January, while Fortress Britain takes the first steps towards the invasion of Europe with the arrival of the first US troop convoy on the Clyde on 26 January 1942.

Above: This Chinese soldier is smiling proudly by his new howitzer. China had joined the Allies following the Japanese attack on the US Navy base at Pearl Harbor in December 1941.

More Japanese troop transports are attacked off Malaya on 26 January. British and Australian air and naval forces have heavy casualties, with thirteen aircraft and two destroyers sunk. The retreating British troops cross the Johor Strait and join the defenders of Singapore. Most of the defences of Singapore face outwards, towards the sea from which the British have expected an attack from since the time Singapore became a British colony. The naval guns facing outwards cannot be turned to face the jungle, from which the Japanese attackers are coming.

Vidkun Quisling becomes prime minister of Norway on 1 February, although power in Norway remains with Berlin. The Kriegsmarine introduce a new naval code too, for communication with their U-boats. It will not be broken before the end of the year but the British will be able to detect U-boats by using radio direction finding to triangulate their positions. The US Navy's carriers *Yorktown* and *Enterprise* make attacks on the Marshall and Gilbert Islands on 1 February. Stalemate has been reached in the desert. The huge distances travelled by both armies have overstretched Nazi supply lines and the troops must wait for fuel, water, ammunition and food. It gives the Allies time to build a new defensive line from Gazala to Bir Hacheim. British forces reject Japan's demands for Singapore to surrender and more British troops are rushed to the 'impregnable' fortress on 4 February. The USA declares war on Thailand on 5 February but ignores Filipino suggestions on the 8th that the country should become independent and that US and Japanese troops should leave. The Japanese continue their onslaught on Singapore, and two Japanese divisions land on 8 February, while the Johor Causeway is repaired and 35,000 Japanese troops and tanks soon cross it from the mainland. The water supply to Singapore is cut on 14 February and, in Britain's greatest defeat of the war, 138,000 men are killed or captured for the loss of 10,000 Japanese. Many more will die in captivity.

In an example of reverse Lend-Lease, on 10 February, Britain offers the United States thirty-four anti-submarine vessels and crews to help counter the German U-boat 'Happy Times' off the coast. Despite the best efforts by the British air force and navy, the German battlecruisers *Scharnhorst* and *Gneisenau*, and the cruiser *Prinz Eugen*, sail up the English Channel from Brest between 11 and 12 February. Forty-two aircraft are shot down and both battlecruisers are damaged by mines. They are easier to contain while in Germany though and *Gneisenau* is hit by a bomb on 26 February, during a raid on Kiel, and is not repaired before the war is over. The day after the successful Channel voyage by the three battleships, Hitler finally admits that Britain will not be invaded and the troops set for Operation Sealion are needed in Russia. The British Bomber Command is set the task of destroying the will of the German people by bombing the heartland of the country. As well as attacking the industry of Germany on a nightly basis, the cities will be attacked too. In Burma, Britain is on the run, and the Battle of the Sittang River sees the British having to abandon their equipment and many troops on the wrong side of the river as the Japanese attack them.

On 19 February, General Dwight D. Eisenhower is placed in charge of the US Army War Plans Division and pushes for the speeding up of Operation Bolero, the transfer of American troops to Britain in preparation for the final assault on Europe. The Asian war is progressing on all fronts. On the 19th, Dutch and US naval vessels fight out the Battle of Lombok Strait, near Bali, with the Japanese navy, while Japanese land- and carrier-based aircraft attack Darwin, in Australia. 172 die as sixteen ships are damaged or sunk in the harbour. In France, the Vichy government tries to take leaders of the 1940 defeat to court on 20 February but the trial soon falters and collapses. It is treated as a joke by many French people. On 22 February, Air Chief Marshal Sir Arthur Harris takes over Bomber Command and begins the process of changing the bomber force with the introduction of new heavy bombers such as the Avro Lancaster and Handley Page Halifax. The Americans bring the war to the Japanese when the USS *Enterprise* leads a task force against Wake Island. Five Allied cruisers and five destroyers are sunk in the Java Sea by Japanese ships with superior firepower and better torpedoes. Japan loses a cruiser and two transports in the fight, which takes place between 27 and 29 February. At Bruneval, near Le Havre, a British assault captures German radar and personnel on 28 February. The equipment captured gives an idea of how far progressed the Germans are with radar.

Another Japanese force, including four aircraft carriers, inflicts severe damage on Allied shipping between 1 and 7 March. Nine warships and ten merchant ships are sunk. On 2 March, all Australian men become liable for war service. The next day, the first raid on Germany takes place by Lancasters, which drop mines in the

Heligoland Bight. The British conscription age is raised on 5 March to include men aged forty-one to forty-five. Britain's troops in Burma abandon Rangoon on 7 March after it is realised the city is untenable. On 9 March, the Dutch East Indies surrender and Japan has completed its goal to create a Southern Resources Area, and now holds mineral and asset rich Malaya and Indonesia. Japan looks at India and Australia.

On 11 March, General MacArthur leaves the Philippines, declaring, 'I shall return'. He becomes C-in-C of US Forces in Australia. In Burma, US General Stilwell takes command of the Chinese Fifth and Sixth armies who are trying to keep the road open for Allied help into China. Nouméa, in New Caledonia, sees an influx of US Seabee engineers, who start the work of constructing a huge American base on the island. A defensive line is created between 13 and 30 March in Burma, from Prome to the Salween River. The Japanese attack on 21 March near Prome and Toungoo. The first American troopships arrive in Australia on 14 March, replacing many Australian troops fighting in Africa and elsewhere. The Italians attack convoys in the Mediterranean on 22-23 March, and only 5,000 of 25,000 tons of goods get through safely after attacks by ship and by air. Lübeck is attacked by Bomber Command on the night of 28/29 March. This is one of the first raids by Lancasters on the German mainland and it begins the shift from industrial to civilian targets, with many of the timber-framed houses of Lübeck destroyed. A raid takes place at Saint-Nazaire by Allied troops. The idea is to destroy the only dry dock large enough to let the *Tirpitz* operate in the Atlantic. 144 die and many are captured. HMS *Campbeltown* is filled with explosives in an attempt to destroy the dock and the gates to it. When she explodes, the damage to the dock gates is severe. With a fear of losing Indian support for a war, the British propose on 29 March to make the country independent at the end of the conflict.

April begins with Japanese attacks on Trincomalee and Colombo in Ceylon. The British fleet is out on patrol but the Japanese still manage to sink numerous vessels between 2 and 8 April. The carrier HMS *Hermes* is lost, as are two heavy cruisers, numerous merchant ships and an Australian destroyer. The final offensives in the Philippines take place between 3 and 9 April. Air and artillery bombardments take place in Bataan, and the American lines are broken on 4 April. 78,000 American and Filipino troops surrender on 9 April, with many enduring a 65-mile forced march with no food or water. Major General Wainwright, the US commander, escapes with around 2,000 troops to Corregidor Island. An offensive begins on 10 April in Burma, with the Japanese attacking after reinforcements have arrived. The Burmese oilfields are taken but have been set alight by the retreating British troops. More Chinese troops flood into Burma in an effort to counter the Japanese attacks but their Sixth Army is overwhelmed on the 23rd. Twelve Lancaster bombers attack Augsburg, and the large diesel engine factory located there, on a daylight raid on 17 April. Seven are lost and the other five are damaged. Another daring raid takes place the day after when Lt-Col. Jimmy Doolittle leads sixteen B-25 Mitchell bombers off from the carrier USS *Hornet* to attack the Japanese mainland. The operation reminds the Japanese that, despite their victories in recent

Above: RAF groundstaff are loading mines on a Lancaster. Built by Avro, the heavy bomber was introduced into service in February 1942 and its primary role was to attack targets within Germany using conventional bombs. Its US counterpart was the B-17 Flying Fortress and over 3,000 of the B-17F variant, which first flew in May 1942, served as the main aircraft of the Eighth Air Force in Europe. Shown below is B-17E *Goonie* in the Pacific theatre, also in 1942.

months, they cannot escape the horrors of war. The bombing convinces them that they must destroy the US Navy in the Pacific. The American bombers overfly Japan and fifteen reach China, with one landing in Siberia. Many of the crews ditch or parachute from their B-25s as they run out of fuel. In the search for Doolittle and his men, the Japanese kill some 250,000 Chinese civilians. Three captured pilots are executed. The first German 'milch cow' supply submarine makes a rendezvous with operational U-boats on 23 April. The replenishment at sea helps double the range of the U-boats. In the first of the so-called Baedeker raids, named after the famous red guidebooks, Exeter is targeted on 24 April in revenge for the attack on Lübeck. The Burma road is cut on 29 April as the Japanese seize the town of Lashio. The Chinese nationalists are now dependent on air supply to keep them armed. The rapid Japanese advances have forced a hurried retreat rather than an organised withdrawal from Burma. The end of the month sees Joseph Stalin declare that Russia has no territorial ambitions other than retaking its own land back.

The road to Mandalay is cut on 1 May and the Japanese capture the city. The Chinese Sixth Army retreats into China and the British are heading for India. A large Japanese force has assembled and is on its way to the Coral Sea as part of the plans to neutralise the American carriers and to take Port Moresby in Papua New Guinea. The US has broken the Japanese code and knows the attacks are on the way. To fool the Japanese into thinking only one aircraft carrier is close, the island of Tulagi in the Solomons is evacuated before it is attacked by the Japanese. On 3 May, Task Force 17, which includes the USS *Hornet*, damages a Japanese destroyer, five aircraft and three minesweepers off Tulagi. Between 5 and 7 May, the British invade Madagascar. The Vichy French island is attacked by a battleship and two aircraft carriers, and the naval base of Diego Suarez surrenders on 7 May. The final days of US and Filipino control of the Philippines are almost over. Corregidor surrenders between 5 and 10 May. 12,495 American and Filipino troops are captured. The campaign has seen 140,000 US and Filipino troops killed or captured for a loss of 4,000 Japanese dead.

The Battle of the Coral Sea continues, with the Japanese and American fleets some 70 miles apart but unable to locate each other. Australian and US cruisers are sent to locate the Port Moresby invasion force but they turn back on 7 May. The US destroyer *Sims* is sunk by Japanese aircraft, and the tanker *Neosho* is scuttled. The Japanese carrier *Shoho* is sunk, as are twenty-one aircraft that try to attack the US fleet. On 8 May, the carrier *Shokaku* is damaged. The *Lexington* is damaged so badly that she is scuttled and the *Yorktown* is also hit. It is the first battle at sea fought exclusively between aircraft carriers. The Japanese lose a small carrier and two are damaged enough that they will not be able to be used at the Battle of Midway. The *Yorktown* is speedily repaired at Pearl Harbor. The attack on Port Moresby has failed and the Japanese have lost many skilled pilots, who will not be replaced. Australia is safe too and, despite air raids and other attacks, the threat to the continent has all but disappeared for the moment.

The war in the Crimea continues and between 8 and 15 May, the German Eleventh Army makes attacks against the Crimean Front. A huge battle around Kharkov sees

'The Fates Decide.' By 1942 the balance had shifted significantly in the Allies' favour, with the US entering the war following the attack on Pearl Harbor in December 1942. This cartoon, published in *Punch*, is by E. H. Shepard who is better known as the illustrator of children's classics such as *Winnie the Pooh* and *The Wind in the Willows*.

the Russians try to surround German units close to the Sea of Azov. The Crimean Kerch Peninsula is captured by the Eleventh Army on 15 May. On 11 May, a last-ditch attempt is made by Commonwealth and British troops to retain Burma at a battle at Kalewa but the Japanese triumph again and the Allies are forced to give up over 80 per cent of Burma. There is good news for the Axis forces in the Mediterranean, when German aircraft sink three British destroyers off Alexandria on the same day. Intelligence reaches the US on 14 May via codebreakers that Japan intends to attack at Midway with the intention of drawing the US Pacific Fleet into battle and destroying it. The British and Commonwealth troops from Burma begin to reach India on 15 May. 13,463 have died! 95,000 Chinese soldiers have been killed too. 5,000-8,000 Japanese soldiers have been killed.

Mexico declares war on Germany, Italy and Japan on 22 May 1942. In Libya, Erwin Rommel's Afrika Korps attacks the Gazala Line on 26 May. Italian tanks attack at Hacheim and are repulsed by Free French forces but the Germans use their tanks more effectively and, despite suffering fuel supply problems, they move forward by 31 May. On 27 May, British-trained Czechoslovakian agents assassinate the German deputy leader in Prague, Czechoslovakia. Reinhard Heydrich is attacked while he is in an open-top car and with no escort. Cologne becomes the first target of the 1,000-bomber raids on 30 May. For a loss of forty aircraft, the British make 59,000 residents of Cologne homeless. The Lancaster had entered service earlier in the year and, on 31 May, the versatile de Havilland Mosquito makes the first of many sorties over Germany in a variety of roles.

Another 1,000-bomber raid is made on Essen on 1 June, with damage caused in the city and the Ruhr valley. In the Pacific, the Japanese attempt to seize Midway in the Hawaiian islands on 4 June. Some 165 vessels are in the Japanese battle and invasion fleets, including eight carriers, but the Americans are aware of the attack and have planned accordingly. A Japanese attack on the Aleutians is ignored as a feint, while the US fleet congregates around Midway. Japan loses three large fleet carriers for the loss of one US carrier and a destroyer. Japan has failed in its attempts to destroy the US fleet, and its losses mean it is now on the defensive in the Pacific. While still managing some gains, it cannot rebuild its air force and ships in time to counter US attacks that it knows are coming. Any hope of a short war has now gone. The siege of Sebastopol sees Germany's Eleventh Army try to wear down the Russian defenders, even using 'Dora', the world's largest siege mortar, against the Russians. Heydrich, the deputy governor of Czechoslovakia, dies on 10 June. He was one of the architects of the Final Solution and took a major part in the Wannsee meeting that saw the Nazis draw up the Final Solution. The German retribution is quick and sees some 3,000 Czech Jews deported; another 1,000 accused of anti-German activities are murdered. The village of Lidice, near Prague, is wiped from the face of the earth immediately after Heydrich is dead, and all its men over fifteen are killed. After the 173 men are executed, the 184 women and 88 children are deported to concentration camps. Many will not return. Lidice is then bulldozed to the ground.

In Libya, the German offensive sees the Free French troops withdraw from Bir Hacheim on 10–11 June and the Afrika Korps is in danger of winning the desert battle. The British withdraw on 13 June. At the Second Washington Conference, on 18 June, Churchill and Roosevelt agree on an invasion of North Africa in 1942, the conditions not being right for an attack on France. The campaign will be code-named Operation Torch. The US and UK also agree to cooperate on nuclear research in an attempt to build a nuclear bomb before the Nazis achieve the same. Bremen is the target for the third 1,000-bomber raid on the 18th, showing the Germans that Britain has the resources to continue the air war on such a scale. Tobruk surrenders to the Germans on 21 June, after the offensive breaks through the desert. Around 30,000 troops and their equipment are captured. The bonus of the Allies' fuel and food sees the Afrika Korps resupplied and they push towards Egypt. The British create a fortified line from El Alamein to the impassable Quattara Depression. The front is held here as the Allies strain the German supply lines. Dwight D. Eisenhower, who will become a post-war US president, takes control of Allied forces in Europe on 25 June. The German summer offensive in Russia begins on 28 June as Army Group South moves from Kursk to Voronezh, which it captures within nine days.

At the beginning of July, Sebastopol finally falls and the Germans capture 90,000 Russian troops. Arctic convoy PQ-17 is ordered to scatter after numerous attacks from the air and U-boat assaults by a whole wolf pack. The escorts withdraw and the thirty-three ships are on their own. Twenty-three of them are sunk and the future of summer convoys is put of hold. The long summer days, with almost no night, make the convoys extremely vulnerable to attack. Hitler orders simultaneous attacks on Stalingrad and the Caucasus on 13 July. This causes huge problems with his overstretched army and the Luftwaffe. The advance towards Stalingrad weakens as Hitler sends the Fourth Panzer Army to the Caucasus. With the forces against Stalingrad and those in the south diverging, it gives the Russians an opportunity to escape. On 23 July, Rostov is captured by the German Army Group A. The army rapidly begins to cross the Caucasus plains.

Hitler moves the Fourth Panzer Army back to the Stalingrad front on 1 August, which then slows down this advance, while removing the Panzer Army from the fight as it relocates and prepares to go back on the offensive again. The 2,200 Japanese soldiers on Guadalcanal island wake up to an attack by the US 1st Marine Division on the morning of 7 August. The airfield the Japanese have been building and from which they could attack Allied sea lanes is captured, as is Tulagi. Despite running low of supplies, the Marines are soon replenished by sea and air. On 9 August, in the Battle of Savo Island, which is next to Guadalcanal, the Japanese damage a cruiser and sink four others. The Japanese have begun to land troops on Guadalcanal in an attempt to throw the Marines back into the sea. Fighting is mainly around the now renamed Henderson Field airstrip. The sea battle is fought mainly at night and the Japanese withdraw, fearing they will be hit by US aircraft. Having lost their defensive cruisers, the US transports leave Guadalcanal and the Marines again have supply problems. In the Mediterranean, Malta is near defeat and between 10 and 15 August, a convoy is sent from Gibraltar to the island.

Despite huge naval support, only four of fourteen ships arrive at the island but they are enough for Malta to survive until the next convoy arrives. The steam tanker *Ohio* is abandoned but recovered and towed into Grand Harbour, where she sinks at her moorings, but not until her precious oil and petrol have been pumped ashore.

Winston Churchill meets with Joseph Stalin on 12 August and Stalin demands a second front to take the pressure from the Russians. On 13 August, Lt-Gen. Bernard Montgomery replaces General Neil Ritchie as commander of the Eighth Army, commonly nicknamed the Desert Rats. Based in East Anglia, the first United States Army Air Force daylight raid on Europe bombs industrial plants in France on 17 August. Two days later, on the 19th, Dieppe is raided by British and Canadian soldiers. 5,000 Canadians, 1,000 British and fifty US troops 'invade' the port. The attempt to create 'reconnaissance in force' fails dismally and 4,000 troops are killed or captured. Between 19 and 24 August, the Germans reach around 30 miles from Stalingrad, where the Russians put up stiff resistance. Brazil declares war on Germany and Italy on 22 August, with their ports now easily accessible to the Allies. Half a world away, in the Solomons, a three-carrier US task force attacks a Japanese convoy headed for Guadalcanal. With four Japanese carriers in the vicinity, the Americans sink one, the *Ryujo*, with ninety aircraft downed too,

Right: Dwight D. Eisenhower was appointed as Commanding General European Theater Operations, United States Army (ETOUSA), on 25 June. The following year he became the Supreme Allied Commander of the Allied Expeditionary Force (SHAEF).

for the loss of seventeen US aircraft and damage to the carrier USS *Enterprise*. The Germans launch an air raid on Stalingrad on 23 August, killing thousands as bombs from 600 aircraft rain down on the city. With supply issues and constant harrying from the air, a German offensive against El Alamein fails as the tanks are damaged in minefields and meet stiff resistance.

2 September is another nightmare day in the history of Europe's Jews. Those who have survived the war so far have been pushed into ghettos in large cities, where they are easier to contain. In Warsaw, today sees the German SS Schutzstaffel (Protection Squads) move into Warsaw's ghetto and force some of the 50,000 inhabitants of this rather crowded area onto trains for the journey to a concentration camp, where they will be gassed or forced into slave labour until they are no longer fit for work. The attempted destruction of an entire religion and all the people who consider it theirs is one of the saddest events of the war. The commander of Army Group A, Field Marshal Wilhelm List, is dismissed by Hitler for criticising his strategy. General von Kleist is his replacement and he continues the siege of Russia's second city, Stalingrad.

Cunard's *Laconia*, used as a troopship, is carrying 1,800 Italian prisoners and Allied troops and their families, when it is sunk on 12 September after being hit by torpedoes from U-156 in the Atlantic. The submarine, realising the ship is full of defenceless people, surfaces and attempts to help as many as possible. An American bomber attacks the U-15, which had stayed close by for two-and-a-half days and had called other U-boats and Vichy French ships to the scene but this just causes the U-156 to slip away, leaving the crew and passengers of the *Laconia* to drown. Many are killed or injured by the B-24 as bombs and strafes the U-boat. Karl Dönitz, the German naval commander, orders his U-boats not to attempt rescue of crew after sinkings. He will be tried at Nuremburg as a result of his order to not let his submarines help shipwrecked sailors.

In Guadalcanal, as the Italians and British bob around the Atlantic awaiting rescue, 6,000 Japanese attempt to capture Henderson Field during the Battle of Bloody Ridge. Despite attacks by wave after wave of Japanese troops, the Marines hold their ground. On 15 September, two Japanese submarines come across an American carrier force transporting troops and supplies to Guadalcanal, sinking the carrier *Wasp* and a destroyer. The much needed troops and supplies get through to Guadalcanal. Another German commander who criticises Hitler's Eastern Front strategy is General Franz Halder, chief of the General Staff. He is replaced by General Kurt Zeitler on 24 September.

In October, the war continues as normal. British air raids on Continental Europe include the first attacks on Turin, Milan and Genoa on the 22nd. The next day, one of the defining battles of the war, the Battle of El Alamein, starts. 195,000 Allied troops face 104,000 Axis soldiers and the battle begins with a fixed artillery barrage, reminiscent of those that pre-empted the fixed battles of the First World War. Much of the preparation for the battle included mass mine clearance in front of the Allied lines, which enabled the Allied forces to push forward soon after the barrage ceased. Rommel is in Germany but quickly returns to the desert to take control. With his arrival, Axis resistance is fierce. The Battle of Santa Cruz on 26 October sees the USS *Hornet* finally sunk. The ship that had carried out the Doolittle Raid was finally sent to the bottom with four Japanese torpedoes after the Japanese found her abandoned. The Americans had tried to sink her but failed after she was fatally wounded in the battle. The Japanese lose the cruiser *Yura,* and the carrier *Shokaku* is badly damaged.

Rommel withdraws from El Alamein at the beginning of November. His troops are running out of supplies. The withdrawal is delayed by Hitler's insistence there should be no withdrawal. The Afrika Korps is pushed back to Tobruk, Benghazi and finally beyond El Agheila on the 24th. The Axis forces under Rommel's control have lost 59,000 dead, wounded or captured. Montgomery's forces have lost 13,000 killed, wounded or missing. It is the first truly major Allied victory against the Germans in the war. The French forces in Madagascar surrender on 5 November. Three days later, Operation Torch begins. Three Allied forces land in Morocco and Algeria, with 34,000 US troops landing near Casablanca, another 39,000 US and British troops coming ashore near Oran and a final 33,000 landing at Algiers. The German and Italian troops in North Africa will soon be under pressure from two sides. As a result of the occupation and quick capitulation of Vichy North Africa, Vichy France itself is invaded by the Germans, beginning on 11 November. All of France is now under the German yoke.

Between 12 and 14 November, in the Solomons, the Americans send a cruiser and destroyer squadron to Guadalcanal, with 11,000 troops. The Japanese navy in the vicinity, some eighteen warships, is severely damaged, with many sunk. Germany is pushing many thousands of reinforcements into North Africa using the short route from Italy to Tunisia. On 17 November, British paratroops land at Souk-el-Arba and join Allied troops heading for Bizerta. By 28 November, the Allies are within shooting distance of Tunis but the Italians and Germans fight back. Bad weather and supply issues stop a major advance by the Allies. On 19 November, the Russian counteroffensive at Stalingrad starts. Ten armies, with 900 tanks, many of them the feared T-34, and 1,100 aircraft attack along a front of 260 miles. The plan is to surround Stalingrad in a pincer movement. The frosty ground helps the mobility of the tanks. The Allied landings in North Africa have taken many Germans from the Eastern Front as Hitler tries to contain the Allies on two fronts. It is the diversion that Stalin is hoping for. By 25 November, the German Sixth Army is trapped and surrounded. Air supply is the only means of getting ammunition, food and other supplies to the beleaguered Germans. Some 320 aircraft make flights constantly into Stalingrad. On 27 November, there is more bad news for Hitler as the French fleet is scuttled in Toulon. Three battleships are among the seventy-two ships and submarines lost to the German war effort. On 30 November, the Americans lose four heavy cruisers at the Battle of Tassafaronga, when five of their cruisers and seven destroyers meet with a Japanese convoy of eight destroyers heading for Guadalcanal. The Japanese only lose one destroyer.

December begins with a report by Sir William Beveridge that sets out a vision for post-war Britain that will include a universal state pension and the first proposals for the National Health Service. The report will set the theme for post-war Britain's social care policies. Meanwhile, in America, on 2 December, the world is changed forever when the world's first controlled nuclear chain reaction takes place. It brings the vision of a nuclear bomb closer. On 6 December, the Germans send two tank columns to try and retake Medjez-el-Bab, which is located around 35 miles south-west of Tunis. Both columns are stopped by artillery fire, aircraft and Allied tanks.

In the Solomons, the Marines are replaced by the US XIV Corps, and General Alexander Patch takes over at Guadalcanal. By the 10th, the Japanese have begun to establish a new front around 6 miles from the perimeter of Henderson Field. The 20,000 Japanese face around 58,000 US troops. Despite their naval losses, the Americans have control of the air around Guadalcanal. December also sees one of the most daring of the Commando raids of the war when ten Marines, commanded by Lt-Col. 'Blondie' Hasler, paddle up the Gironde to attack German shipping at Bordeaux. Numerous ships are sunk by the four canoeists who reach the port, but only Hasler and 'Sparks', his number two, survive the mission. In the south of Russia, Field Marshal von Manstein tries to relieve the Sixth Army in Stalingrad. Army Group Don manages to get to within 35 miles of Stalingrad but fuel shortages see the attempt to reach the besieged Sixth Army fail. By the end of the month, in the deep Russian winter, von Manstein's relief force is pushed back, and the men of the Sixth Army endure terrible conditions and lack of food and supplies as the Russians constantly attack them. On Christmas Eve, Vichy French Admiral Darlan, who gave the surrender of North Africa to the Allies, is shot dead by a Vichy supporter. In the Barents Sea a battle is fought between the pocket battleship *Lützow*, cruiser Admiral Hipper and six destroyers of the German navy and the escorts of Convoy JW-51B. The Germans are cautious; they have been ordered to be so and the British use this to their advantage. Each side loses a destroyer but the German leader is furious. The large number of sailors and support tied up by the German navy generate little results and the Battle of the Barents Sea leads to the end of major action by the German surface fleet.

1941 ended with the Allies being attacked on all sides and 1942 sees the first year of real successes for the British and Americans. By waking the Russian Bear, Germany will ultimately lose the war, a war it cannot fight on two fronts. The Americans have been woken from their isolationist ideals and have come into the war with gusto. The Japanese have failed, almost as they have begun the war, with the loss of irreplaceable aircraft carriers and aircraft, as well as pilots and support crews. The saddest event of the year has been the meeting in Wannsee that sets out the Final Solution and will see the needless murder of some 6 million innocent people, whose only crime has been that of race or religion. The atom bomb is one step closer to being created, and both Britain and America will ensure the weapon is ready for use by 1945. The new year will see the Allies make more victories and will be the true turning point for both Japanese and Germans, with defeats in the Pacific and in Russia, while Italy will be invaded and the Allies once more have a toehold in Europe, albeit in the boot of Italy.

JANUARY 1942

A British Crusader encounters the traditional ship of the desert in Libya. The Crusader was widely considered to be the most important British tank to participate in the North Africa campaign, but by the end of 1942 the lack of an armaments upgrade left it ill-matched against the Afrika Korp's newly introduced Tiger tank and it was largely superseded by the US-built M3 Grant and ubiquitous M4 Sherman.

Above: Winston Churchill wearing his one-piece siren suit, and at the controls of a Boeing 314 Clipper. At the end of 1941 the Prime Minister and his entourage of Chiefs of Staff had travelled to Washington for discussions with President Roosevelt. While in the USA he was flown to a meeting of the Bermuda Assembly aboard the flying boat, and his arrival in Bermuda is shown below. Churchill had been scheduled to return by sea on HMS *Duke of York*, but decided instead to fly back to Britain on the flying boat, making the crossing on 16 January 1942.

1942 began badly for the Axis powers in North Africa.

Above: Prisoners, mostly men of the Afrika Korps, gathered on the shore at Tobruk to await transport by sea to prisoner-of-war camps. In the operations that resulted in the surrender of Bardia, Sollum and Halfaya, about 14,000 Germans and Italians were captured.

Right: The 'Desert Fox', Erwin Rommel, is regarded as one of the most professional and accomplished of the German field marshals of the Second World War. In February 1941 he had been appointed as commander of the Deutsches Afrikakorps (DKA), and despite the loss of territory at the start of 1942 he would respond with a highly effective counter-attack in the summer.

Above: German soldiers surrender to New Zealand troops in January 1942. A wounded prisoner is riding in the Bren Carrier. *Below:* An enemy mobile gun which has been put out of action by British artillery. In the foreground lies the body of the Italian gunner.

Above: On the waterfront at Bardia the German and Italian prisoners are being taken to a concentration point. The commander of the garrison, Major-General Schmidt, had surrendered to the British on 2 January 1942.

Right: These disks are German 'Teller' anti-tank mines which the South African sappers disarm and remove from a minefield laid outside Bardia.

Two views of a de Havilland Dragon Rapide ambulance aircraft operated by the Royal Australian Air Force to ferry the wounded between the advanced dressing stations in the desert and base hospitals in Libya. In theory the Red Cross emblem, visible in the upper image, should have ensured immunity from attack, but unfortunately this did not prove to be the case when it was attacked by Messerschmitts.

Above: More biplanes over Libya, this time Fairey Albacores of the Fleet Air Arm. This torpedo-carrying dive-bomber and reconnaissance aircraft operated both from carriers and land bases. Introduced in 1940, the Albacore was to have been a replacement for the ageing Swordfish, but already looking outmoded by 1942 it was withdrawn in 1944. *Below:* South African crew of a US-built Douglas Boston III leaving their aircraft after a desert patrol, also in Libya.

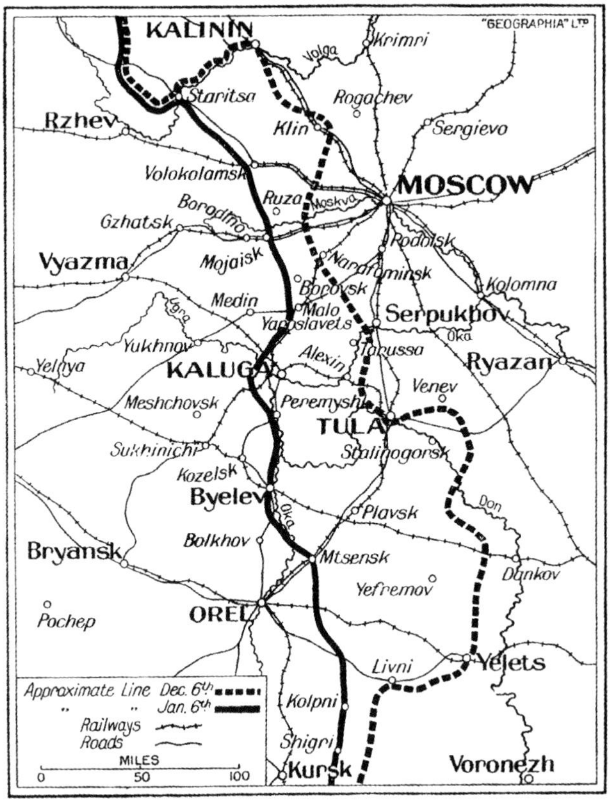

The Russians began 1942 in a bullish mood when Joseph Stalin ordered a general offensive on the so-called German 'winter line' on 5 January. The Germans were unprepared for the counter-attack so early in the year and initial successes saw the capture of their transport, food, ammunition and weapons. But it wasn't long before the Germans were holding their own, using new defensive tactics to contain the Russian assault.

Left: Map showing the movement of the front line near Moscow by 6 January.

Below: One of the heavily armoured Kliment Voroshilov KV-1 tanks, named after the Soviet defence commissar, shown on the streets of Moscow.

Above left: A Russian hero, Major Laptev, recounts how he silenced six batteries of enemy guns. *Above right:* An RAF officer with a Soviet Air Force captain takes observations under the watch of a protective guard. *Below:* General Sikorski, Poland's leader, shakes hand with Molotov, the Soviet Commissar for Foreign Affairs, to herald a new relationship between the two countries.

Top: A Cossack cavalry division charging over the snow towards German lines. *Middle:* A party of volunteers from Leningrad on reconnaissance patrol, concealing themselves behind the banks of a river. *Bottom:* Soviet anti-tank gun.

Above: Truckloads of Red Army troops passing through Moscow. They are reinforcements for the men who broke through the German fortifications at Mozhaysk. *Below:* In the wintry conditions these soldiers are ranging a mine-thrower and are on the point of firing.

Above: Chasing the German stragglers at Rostov-on-Don where the invasion was finally turned into a retreat. Rostov-on-Don was crucially important as the gateway to the mineral and oil wealth of the Caucasus – see page 113. *Below:* A German tank lies abandoned by the roadside. The Russians were far more experienced in dealing with harsh wintry conditions.

Top: Young Soviet engineers working on an armoured train that was their 'gift' to the Red Army. *Bottom:* In many ways the socialist ethic suited the needs of war and civilians are shown putting their backs into clearing snow from the railway tracks in order to reopen communications with the east. This scene is near a station on the Dzerzhinsky Railway.

Top left: A Chinese soldier displays captured Japanese equipment, including respirator, rifle and steel helmet. *Top right:* Some of the 2,000 Japanese prisoners taken at Changsha. Here the Japanese had launched their first major offensive into China, but by January 1942 it was failing and the Chinese inflicted heavy losses. *Bottom:* A Chinese machine-gunner takes a sight.

The Japanese forces were having greater success in other areas of the Far East conflict.

Right: A rubber factory burns during the Japanese advance through Malaya, part of the scorched earth policy. The capital, Kuala Lumpur, fell to the Japanese on 12 January 1942.

Above: Japanese invasion money issued in Malaya.

Right: Sikh soldiers with a field gun. By the end of January the Allied forces were leaving Malaya and retreating south to Singapore. On the 31st they blew a 70-foot hole in the causeway linking Johor with Singapore.

Top left: Argyll and Sutherland Highlanders with an armoured car. This is one of the big Lanchester 6x4 vehicles that saw action in the Battle of Malaya.

Left: The rough terrain in Malaya made land operations difficult and aircraft played an important part. Here a Bristol Blenheim is being uncrated. The Blenheims had arrived in 1941.

Below: Royal Australian Air Force (RAAF) Hudsons flying over Malaya. There were four Australian squadrons operating in the country under RAF Command. During the Japanese invasion these aircraft provided aerial reconnaissance as well as attacking the enemy.

FEBRUARY 1942

On 12 February 1942, the German battleships *Scharnhorst* and *Gneisenau*, together with the cruiser *Prinz Eugen*, made a dash from Brest and eastwards through the Channel to the German bases on the North Sea. Leading the attack against the German vessels was the Royal Navy destroyer *Campbell*, shown above, which got close enough to release her torpedoes. The German ships did make it, despite a number of hits by RAF Blenheim bombers.

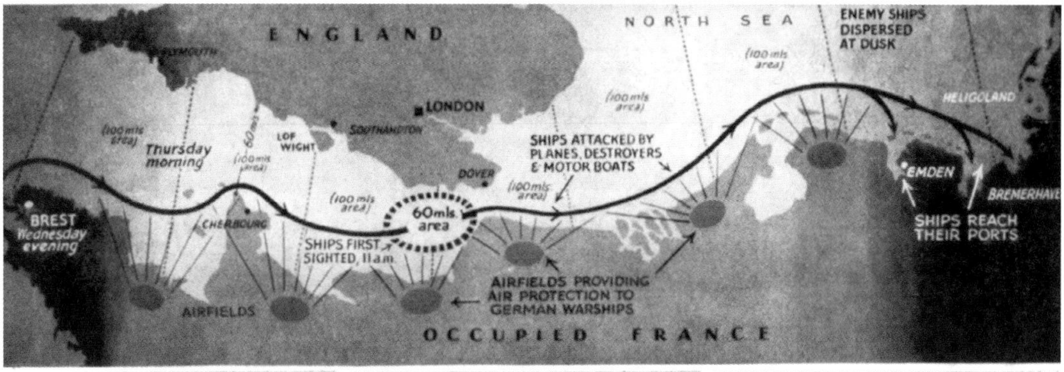

On 12 February 1942, the German battleships *Scharnhorst* and *Gneisenau*, along with the 10,000-ton cruiser *Prinz Eugen*, made a dash from Brest to German bases during which they were attacked by British bombers, torpedo-carrying aircraft, destroyers and motor torpedo-boats. This montage shows the course they followed, and some of the men involved in the pursuit. At the bottom is the crew of one of the destroyers involved in the attack.

Right: Map showing the areas where British troops fought to stem the tide of the Japanese advance. By the end of January they had been forced to abandon the Malayan Peninsula, and on 4 February the British rejected Japanese demands for the surrender of Singapore. It was thought that Singapore was impregnable to attack.

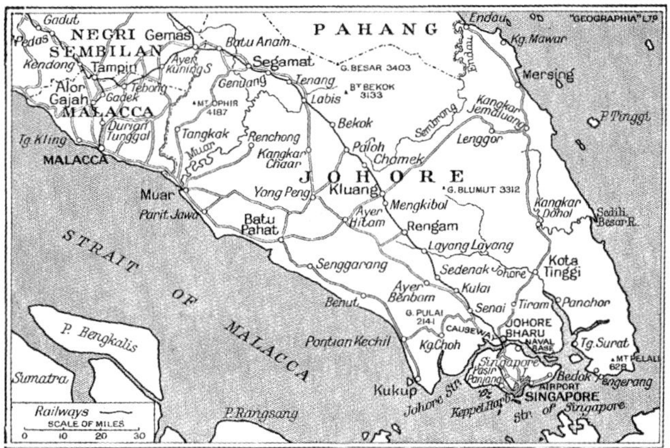

Above: Japanese forces landed on the north-west of the island, the causeway from Johor was repaired, and with control of the air, Singapore was overwhelmed. Lieutenant General Sir Arthur Percival's surrender on 14 February was one of Britain's greatest defeats of the war.

Right: Indian troops in Singapore had fought alongside the British and Commonwealth forces which lost 138,000 men in the Malayan Peninsula. Thousands more would die in captivity.

In the last days before the arrival of the Japanese, inhabitants of Singapore look on as members of an Air Raid Precautions team demonstrate the method for dealing with an incendiary device. The exercise is taking place in front of De Vere's in Singapore's famous Raffles Place.

Above: British armoured cars line up in Singapore in January 1942. *Below:* The smoke billowing in the distance heralds the advance of the Japanese into Singapore.

Above left: The locals dug trenches in the town to defend against a Japanese invasion. *Above right:* A Singapore rescue squad at work clearing up the wreckage in a suburban area.

This corner of a square in Singapore has received a direct hit from a Japanese bomb.

Above: The French liner *Normandie*, once the holder of the Blue Riband, had been docked in New York harbour when, on 9 February 1942, she was set alight by stray sparks from a workman's oxyacetylene torch. Taken over by the US government, the ship was being fitted out as a troopship. After the fire had been extinguished the *Normandie* toppled over in about 50 feet of water. She was later salvaged at great expense, to be finally scrapped in 1946.

'Bomber' Harris was the architect of the great and highly contoversial wartime experiment of strategic bombing. Put in charge of Bomber Command, in 1942 he persuaded the British Cabinet to approve 'area bombing' of German cities in preference to target bombing of individual sites. 'The Nazis entered this war under the rather childish delusion that they were going to bomb everyone else, and nobody was going to bomb them. At Rotterdam, London, Warsaw and half a hundred other places, they put their rather naive theory into operation. They sowed the wind, and now they are going to reap the whirlwind.'

Left: Cover of the official Air Ministry account of Bomber Command's earlier wartime activities, published by HMSO in 1941.

Above: A busy scene at a factory producing Rolls-Royce Merlin XX aero engines. *Below:* This is Mary Devlin, an Irish worker in a Canadian factory, turning components for Bren guns.

29
28
27

Over 12,000 B-17 Flying Fortresses were built at the Boeing plant in Seattle and also at Lockheed Vega, Burbank, California, and Douglas Aircraft at Long Beach, California. Of these the B-17G was the most prolific model, with 8,680 produced.

These dramatic photographs show B-17s in production and were taken for an American magazine. The aircraft were built using highly efficient production line methods, a system adopted by the other Allies. Note the integration of male and female workers.

Right: Scenes at Boeing's Seattle factory.

Opposite page: Tail sections lined up at Long Beach.

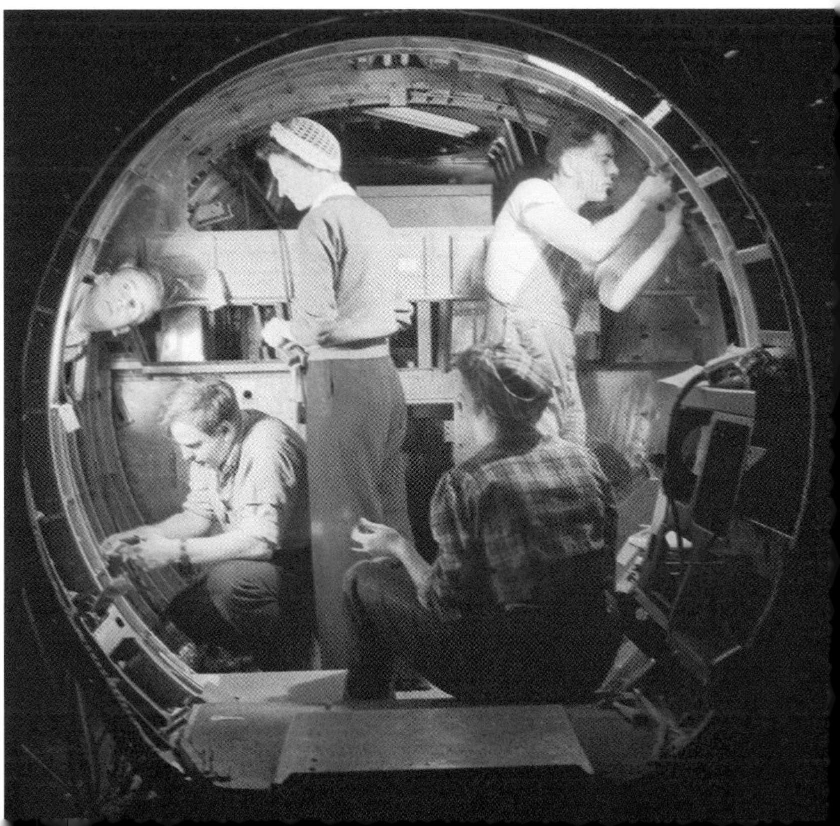

Above: The North American Aviation P-51 Mustang was developed as a long-range fighter-bomber, and would serve extensively as an escort for the heavy bombers. It first flew in October 1940 and was introduced into service in 1942. Four Mustang squadrons provided tactical reconnaissance for the ground troops at Dieppe.

Left: A formation of Grumman TBF Avengers (the TBM designation was used for those built by General Motors). A torpedo bomber, it was developed for the US Navy and Marine Corps initially. Entering service in 1942, the Avenger first saw action at the Battle of Midway in June.

MARCH 1942

During a tour of a US bomber squadron based in England, the King inspected the crew of B-17 Flying Fortress *Holey Joe*.

Above: A vast amount of war material was convoyed over the Pacific from the USA to Australia. These American troops were stationed in the continent to defend against Japanese invaders.

Right: Wrecked lorries amid the ruins of the Renault factory at Île Seguin, Paris, bombed on 3 March 1942.

Opposite page: A scene from what had once been the tennis deck of a passenger liner, now being used for conveying American troops and supplies across the Atlantic.

Above: The Red Army's ubiquitous medium tank, the T-34, is shown providing cover and support for the infantry. Sometimes the tanks were also used to transport small units of infantrymen riding on their upper surfaces.

The T-34 Medium Tank

It has been described as the most effective and influential tank design of the Second World War. Having first entered service in 1940, the T-34 medium-tank went on to become the mainstay of the Soviet armed forces throughout the remainder of the war and it was essential in stemming the German offensive on the Eastern Front in the summer of 1942.

The initial armament was a powerful 76.2-mm gun, but a second version, the T-34-85, followed in 1944 and boasted the larger 85-mm gun to deal with Germany's latest big tanks. Throughout its production the design of the T-34 was continuously refined, both in terms of its performance and to reduce the manufacturing costs. Together these factors made it the most-produced tank of the entire war. By the time production had finally ceased in 1958, Soviet factories had turned out a staggering 84,070 T-34 tanks in its variants. During the war the sub-assemblies, engines and other components of the T-34 were produced at a number of different factories in Leningrad, Moscow, Stalingrad and Gorky.

Above left: Red Army troops with automatic rifles attacking a section of German-held railway line. *Above right:* Street fighting in a village near Kharkov. *Below:* Earlier in the year the German forces had dug themselves in to hold back the Russians, but in the summer they would be mounting an effective counteroffensive to regain lost ground.

Above: An underground Soviet weapons factory built into the cliffs at Sevastopol. The British and Germans both used underground facilities to hide and protect production facilities. *Below:* A captured German reconnaissance aircraft exhibited at the Central House of the Red Army.

Opposite page: Alexander Yakolev's Yak-1 fighter being mass-produced in a Russian factory in 1942. The Yak-1 was everything you could possibly want in a fighter aircraft. It was fast, manoeuvrable, well armed and easy to maintain. 8,700 were built in three variants.

This unusual armoured car was used by the Russians as a mobile reconnaissance post, probing the woods to find enemy positions.

Captured by the Russians, a German 15-cm heavy infantry howitzer mounted on self-propelled tracks for greater mobility. Similar machines had been deployed in the Libyan desert.

Russian supply roads in Iran. *Above:* Railway rolling stock shipped from Britain. Christened 'Churchill's Reply', the trains are preparing to move north from the marshalling yards at Ahwaz, in Iran, and along the Trans-Iranian line to Russia. *Below:* A motor column transports war supplies across the marsh and desert to Ahwaz to link up with the trains. Altogether the journey could take up to eight days to complete.

Building the 'Atlantic Bridge' – RAF Ferry Command

As American factories geared up their output, new methods of getting the aircraft to Europe had to be devised. In general, only the smaller aircraft were suitable for transportation by ship, and even then it was a slow and hazardous journey with the U-boats exacting a heavy toll on transatlantic shipping. What was needed was a 'bridge' for the traffic of war and it was George Woods Humphrey, the managing director of Imperial Airways, who had proposed a solution back in 1940: ferrying the aircraft by air, provided that he could muster enough of the old transatlantic pilots together. At that time the USA had yet to enter the war, although it was building aircraft under the Lend-Lease arrangement, and accordingly he arranged with Canadian Pacific in Montreal to use their facilities. On 14 November 1940, seven twin-engined Hudsons, crewed by Canadian personnel, made the non-stop crossing. This laid the foundations of what was to become RAF Ferry Command.

The original band of Imperial Airway's pilots was added to by RAF and Royal Canadian Air Force pilots, augmented by a motley gang of civilians – cropdusters, skywriters, barnstormers and other commercial flyers – to form the backbone of the delivery service across both the Atlantic and, later on, the Pacific oceans. The flights were often made in challenging conditions, but the Ferrymen kept flying even when other aircraft were confined to the ground. Having reached their destination, usually England, most pilots returned by ship initially, but this caused delays of up to two weeks and later on, to increase efficiency, the Return Ferry Service was established using converted Liberators to fly the ferry crews back.

By 1942 RAF Ferry Command was delivering a steady flow of aircraft across the Atlantic. *Top:* Inside the control at Prestwick where RAF officers watch for the arrival of an aircraft. *Bottom:* In the nerve centre of RAF Ferry Command the hourly position of each aircraft is plotted by the WAAF corporal on duty. *Opposite page:* US personnel inspecting and servicing Lockheed Hudsons prior to their transatlantic delivery flight to the UK.

Above: The first of the so-called Tuskegee airmen – a name given to a group of African-American pilots who served with 332nd Fighter Group and the 447th Bombardment Group of the USAAF. They are shown during training in 1942. *Below:* Mechanics servicing the undercarriage of a B-17 Flying Fortress in the South Pacific.

APRIL 1942

Damaged by shellfire from the Italian battleship *Littorio* at the Second Battle of Sirte on 22 March 1942, HMS *Kingston* was taken into dry dock in La Valletta harbour, Malta, for repairs. The K Class destroyer was attacked by German aircraft and on 11 April she was struck a fatal blow amidships, and rolled over in the dock. The following year, the ship was split in two, and the two halves floated out of the dock in preparation for scrapping.

The main thrust of the Japanese offensive to seize Burma, which was under the rule of the British, began in April 1942. The map, above left, shows the area of fighting in the upper part of the country. *Above right:* A supply column in India. *Below:* This Burmese village has been bombed by the Japanese to create panic and drive the local population into the jungle.

Burma had something the Japanese wanted: oil. *Above:* The oilfields at Yenangyaung were set alight by the British to prevent them falling into Japanese hands. *Below:* Another scene of destruction as electrical machinery is piled up in a pit that will be flooded with oil and burned. An oil tank is already blazing in the background, sending up a pall of black smoke.

On the road to Rangoon (known nowadays as Yangon). *Above:* Local transport facilities and labour were employed by the Japanese in their advance to Rangoon. *Below:* General Yamashita, in the foreground, who was Commander-in-Chief of all Japanese forces in the Malayan campaign, inspects newly captured territory with an entourage of staff officers.

Above left: In the south-west of China, a Chinese anti-aircraft gunner at Chungking is on the watch for Japanese aircraft using range-find apparatus. *Above right:* Swinging a sound detector into position to give warning of approaching aircraft. Although the Chinese were on the Allied side, the equipment is clearly of German origin.

Above: A British newsreel picture of Chinese troops entering a Burmese village. The Japanese wanted to gain control of Burma and use it as a base for an attack on India which, if successful, would have cut off the supply routes of Allied war supplies to the Chinese.

Above: US Lieutenant General Stilwell – 'Vinegar Joe' – shown inspecting a motor school at the Chinese-American training centre in India. *Below:* These Chinese troops are firing a German-built 7.5-cm infantry howitzer.

Looking down the deck of the Japanese carrier *Akagi* during flight operations as part of the Indian Ocean raid in March and April 1942. On 9 April her D3A and Zero aircraft participated in the attack that sunk both the *Hermes*, a small aircraft carrier, and its escort, the Australian destroyer *Vampire*. The *Akagi* would see further action in the Battle of Midway.

The German vengeance raids on British historic cities were known as the 'Baedeker Raids' after the German guidebooks of that name.

Above left: Exeter was bombed on the night of 23/24 April 1942.

Above right: Extensive damage inflicted on a 'North Midland town' on 28 April.

Left: A bomb fell on the south choir aisle of Exeter Cathedral, demolishing St James's Chapel and the sacristy.

Opposite page, main picture: The Guildhall in York burns on the night of 28 April.

Opposite page, inset: Norwich was attacked on 26 April. This is the Old Boar's Head, a famous landmark in the city.

Above: Indian troops at Alexandria watching, on 11 April 1942, the arrival of the hospital ship *Llandovery Castle* bringing South African, Indian, New Zealand, Australian and British wounded prisoners of war from Smyrna, where they had been exchanged for Italians. *Below:* Some of the returning prisoners at Cairo. In exchange for 919 Italians, the *Llandovery Castle* brought fifty-nine sick and wounded British troops to Alexandria.

MAY 1942

On 15 May 1942 the Crown Colony-Class cruiser HMS *Trinidad* was attacked by German Ju 88 dive-bombers while serving in the Arctic escorting the PQ-13 convoy that was taking Allied war supplies to Russia. Although only one bomb hit the ship it was enough to start a serious fire, and severely damaged, she was scuttled, with a torpedo from HMS *Matchless* completing the task.

With the Japanese submarines harassing the British Eastern Fleet in the Indian Ocean, the Vichy France colony of Madagascar became of strategic importance to both sides, with the possibility of the Japanese using the islands as a base. On 5 May 1942, the British launched Operation Ironclad to seize the northern port of Diego Suarez, and in the subsequent campaign, between 10 September and 6 November, they seized control of the entire island. *Above:* Troops landing on the west coast of Madagascar at Majunga Quay. *Below:* As the British advanced they found that much of the transport infrastructure had been systematically wrecked. Here they are landing a light locomotive at Brickaville.

Reinhard Heydrich, left, was one of the main architects of the Final Solution – see page 130. On 27 May 1942 Heydrich was attacked on the streets of Prague by a team of Czech and Slovak soldiers trained by the British, and died of his injuries a week later. In retaliation, and on Hitler's orders, at least 1,300 Czechs were executed. *Above:* A stamp featuring Heydrich's death mask. *Below:* An illustration of the assassination in Prague.

On 18 April 1942, sixteen B-25B Mitchell medium-bombers, shown above, took off from the US carrier *Hornet* to mount an audacious raid on Tokyo and other targets within Japan itself. In part this was in retaliation for the attack on Pearl Harbor, but it was also a demonstration that the Japanese Home Islands were not beyond the reach of American aircraft. *Below:* Lieutenant Colonel 'Jimmy' Doolittle, who planned and led the raid, and some of the aircrew.

Above: B-25 taking off from USS *Hornet* at the start of the Doolittle raid. As the Mitchells were too big to land back on the carrier the plan was to attack Japan and then fly on to land in China. *Below:* Eight of the Americans were captured by the Japanese army in China and executed. In addition it is estimated that 250,000 Chinese civilians and soldiers died in the massive Japanese operation to find the missing aircrew and punish those who had aided the Americans.

Here come the Yanks. *Above:* B-17 ready for flight testing at Boeing's facility in Seattle. The first US units operating the B-17 in England arrived at Great Missenden in May 1942. *Below:* Boston aircraft of RAF Bomber Command flying over Le Havre docks on a daylight raid, 16 April 1942. In the photograph one bomb (shown as A) is exploding across the dock gates, and several have struck the barges on the dockside (B).

Above: Aircrew of the Boston IIIs with the station commander in the operations room prior to a flight. Every detail of the target, the route to be taken and the method of approach are discussed in detail before they take off on their mission. *Below:* Air-to-air photograph of Boston IIIs in flight. In 1942 the pilots and crew of RAF Bomber Command carried out a series of bold daylight attacks in Germany and in German-occupied territory.

Above: Return from a sweep over enemy-occupied territory. The Third American Eagle Fighter Squadron, with British and Allied pilots, attacked the docks at Ostend and set fire to industrial plants at Zeebrugge. Here an American pilot is shown leaving his Spitfire after the sweep. *Below:* A Hurricane bomber is being loaded with bombs for another mission across the Channel.

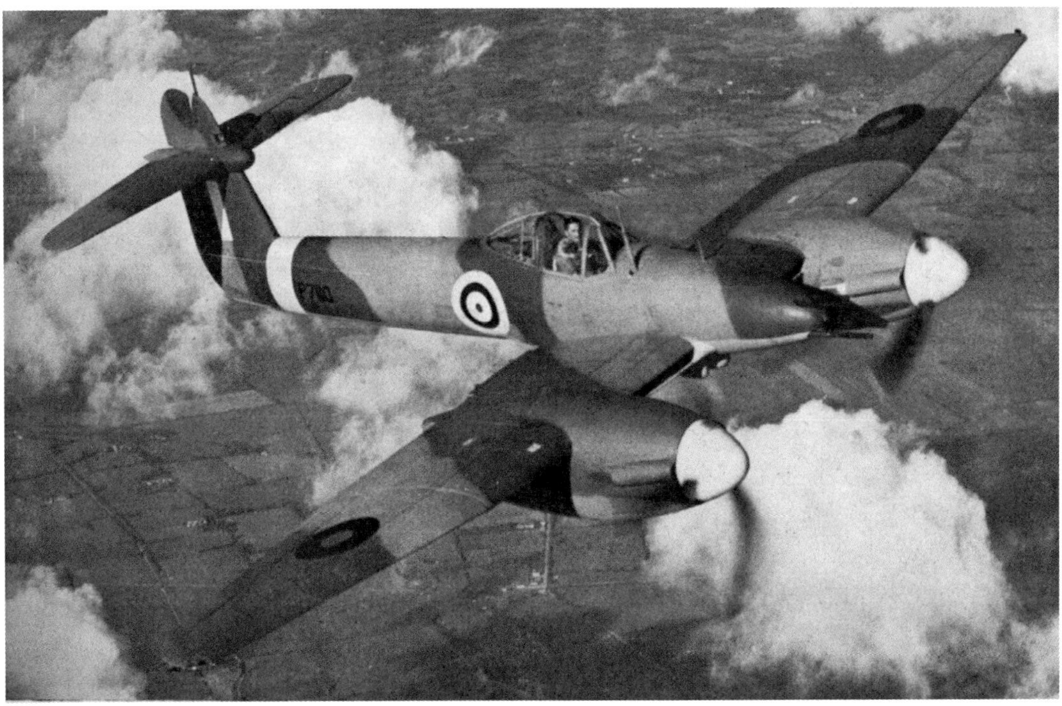

Above: The Westland Whirlwind was a fast aircraft, and with its nose bristling with four 20-mm cannon it certainly looked the business. This twin-engined heavy-fighter was developed by Westland Aircraft. It first flew in October 1938 and was introduced into service in June 1940, a delay caused by protracted problems with the Rolls-Royce Peregrine engines. In the event, only 116 Whirlwinds were built and it was withdrawn in 1943.

Left: A load of 2,000-lb bombs being run up to a Manchester bomber. The twin-engined Avro 679 Manchester had been introduced into service as a heavy bomber in 1940 and served with the RAF and the Canadian Air Force. Deemed a failure because it was underpowered, it was retired in 1942. The Manchester was the direct forerunner of the four-engined Lancaster. *Below:* RAF ground crew move a Stirling bomber the hard way. The Short Stirling had a relatively brief career, being relegated to secondary duties, such as a transport aircraft and glider tug, in 1943. *Opposite:* Inside a Stirling's cockpit with the bomber-aimer emerging from his compartment.

The Avro Lancaster first saw service with RAF Bomber Command in 1942. This four-engine heavy-bomber quickly became the main aircraft in the RAF's stategic bomber offensive in Europe – see page 42. Powered by four Rolls-Royce Merlins in most versions, over 7,000 Lancs were built. Its large unobstructed bomb bay meant that it could carry the largest bombs available, ultimately including the 22,000-lb Grand Slam. *Below:* Evidence of damage caused by an RAF raid on the Heinkel facility at Rostock, in northern Germany, in 1942.

The role of the Allied bombing campaign was not only to inflict direct damage on the German war industry and to disrupt the transport infrastructure, it was also about diverting valuable resources into ever more elaborate defensive measures.

Top right: The heavily fortified U-boat pens on France's Atlantic coast were built by the Organisation Todt using local and slave labour.

Middle right: This exhibition hall on the Kaiserdam in Berlin has been covered with huge camouflage nets to conceal its distinctive outline.

Bottom right: More deception in Berlin. The main east–west road through the city is under a canopy of green foliage and spruce trees intended to break up the clear lines of the highway by creating the illusion of areas of parks or woodland.

The Luftwaffe's bombing raids on English cities continued through May 1942. The images on this page show the damage caused at Canterbury by the night raids of 31 May. *Above:* The ruins of a bombed school and, on the right, residents salvaging a few personal belongings from the rubble. *Below:* Firefighters at work, damping down the fires in Canterbury.

JUNE 1942

Free French anti-aircraft gunners in North Africa. Led by de Gaulle, the Free French forces continued to fight on the side of the Allies after the fall of France.

USS *Yorktown* was badly damaged at the Battle of the Coral Sea but was speedily repaired and reappeared unexpectedly for the Battle of Midway, where she was finally met her end. Despite huge efforts to salvage her after enemy attacks, she eventually rolled over and sank with the loss of 141 crew.

The Battle of Midway

Six months after Pearl Harbor and the sinking of numerous American ships in a surprise attack designed to disable the American Pacific fleet, the Japanese navy was soundly defeated at a small Pacific island called Midway Atoll. The battle came barely a month after the Americans had lost the Battle of the Coral Sea, where the aircraft carrier *Lexington* had been sunk and the *Yorktown* so badly damaged that the Japanese thought it had been lost too.

Like all plans, it seemed foolproof! The Japanese intended to lure the American aircraft carriers that they had not succeeded in destroying at Pearl Harbor into a trap, destroying them and hoping to knock America out of the war, while giving Japan the ability to expand its sphere of influence in the Pacific. The capture of Midway Atoll and its airfield would also prevent American attacks on Japan itself. On 18 April 1942, Jimmy Doolittle's B-25 bombers had flown from USS *Hornet* to attack Tokyo and other targets on the Japanese island of Honshu, providing a valuable morale boost to the USA and showing the Japanese that their homeland was not invulnerable to attack. Midway was to be the victory battle of the war for the Japanese, who had placed their whole nation's future on a quick campaign that would prevent the USA from building up enough resources to wipe them out. The capture of Midway would also be the prelude to attacks on Fiji and Samoa, and would give the Japanese the ability to attack Hawaii, denying the islands as a base to the USA. Little did the Japanese know that their plan was doomed to failure.

Failure was inevitable, not only because the Japanese were unprepared for the battle, but also because the Americans had broken their naval cipher, giving the US Navy prior warning of the attack, but also allowing them to prepare a trap for the Japanese ships.

Japan had quickly realised its initial territorial ambitions in South East Asia. Hong Kong, Singapore, the Philippines and Indonesia had all been taken quite speedily and now it was looking to expand its zone of influence. Midway was chosen for the clash of the two nations as it was at the end of the Hawaiian chain of islands, but still some 1,300 miles from Oahu and Pearl Harbor. The Americans would choose to fight to retain Midway. They had no choice! The Japanese assumed that the US Navy only had two aircraft carriers available, the *Hornet* and the *Enterprise*, little knowing that *Yorktown* was hurriedly being repaired in Pearl Harbor and would make an important contribution to the upcoming battle. Yamamoto, the Japanese Admiral in charge of the planning, also assumed that the Americans had no fight left in them after six months of terrible defeats and disasters. To deceive the Americans, the Japanese fleets were kept a distance apart, so their strength could not be ascertained. This brought with it a challenge in that the Japanese fleets could not support each other. Japanese attacks on the Aleutians also took forces away from the battle fleet sailing for Midway. These could have caused the battle to be lost, but the main reason the Japanese were defeated at Midway was the breaking of their naval code. Yamamoto was not aware that the Americans knew of their plans. It meant, too, that the Americans knew of both attacks and knew that the Japanese carrier force was split between the Aleutians and Midway.

The *Yorktown*, fresh from the Battle of the Coral Sea, had sailed to Pearl Harbor, was hastily repaired in less than seventy-two hours, then provisioned and set sail for Midway, despite not being fully operational. By 4 June, the USAAF and Marine Corps had some 126 aircraft stationed at Midway. Many were obsolete but the numbers were hopefully enough. The Japanese had lost an aircraft carrier during the Battle of the Coral Sea and another suffered enough damage to be dry-docked and unavailable. Another undamaged carrier was in Kure awaiting replacement aircraft and pilots, after losing around half of her air group. Only four carriers were available for Midway: *Kaga, Akagi, Hiryū and Sōryū.* The Japanese were unaware that the American aircraft carriers were not at Pearl, as their submarines arrived too late off Midway to detect them and aircraft could not spy on Pearl as the French Frigate Shoals that they had used previously to refuel were occupied by American warships. A new Japanese code had not been implemented until days before the battle and the Americans knew all about the attack and the disposition of the Japanese ships and aircraft. They had discovered the attack was at Midway and had planned accordingly.

At around 0900 on 3 June, a PYB Catalina found the Japanese Occupation Fleet about 580 miles west-south-west of Midway. Three hours later, the transport fleet was found about the same distance west of Midway. B-17s were sent off to attack the first force but none hit their mark and little damage was reported. Early on 4 June, a Japanese tanker was sunk by a PYB Catalina at around 0100, the only

Below: The American flat-tops had wooden decks, unlike the armoured versions on British ones. This made them vulnerable to attack. A flight of bombers is readied for take off on USS *Enterprise* during the Battle of Midway.

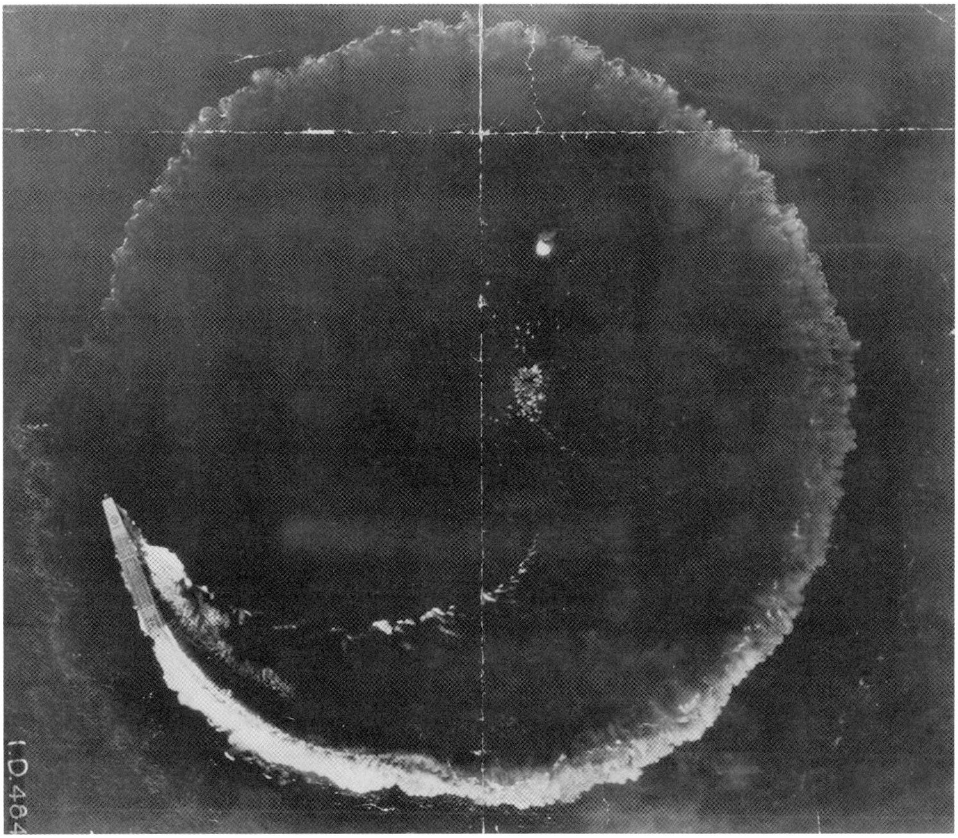

Above: A Japanese flat-top, photographed by the crew of a B-17, as it attempts to evade the bombs and torpedoes of the American craft.

successful torpedo attack by an American aircraft during the battle. At 0430, the first Japanese flights took off for Midway. Thirty-six dive-bombers, thirty-six torpedo bombers and the same number of Mitsubishi Zero fighters set course for Midway. Eleven of Midway's PYBs set off at the same time as the Japanese strike force in an effort to search for the Japanese carriers. At 0530, two flat-tops with empty decks were spotted. The Americans knew the attack was on its way and sent off unescorted bombers to destroy the Japanese carriers. The fighters remained behind to protect Midway, which detected the incoming Japanese aircraft minutes before they attacked at 0620. Midway was bombed and badly damaged. The Midway-based Marine fighters suffered huge losses as they intercepted the Japanese aircraft. Four B5Ns were destroyed and three Zeros too, but the Marines lost sixteen aircraft. Heavy anti-aircraft fire downed four more Japanese aircraft, damaging many more. As a result of the initial attack, only two American fighters remained at Midway in operational condition. Over 10 percent of the Japanese force was destroyed (eleven aircraft), with fourteen badly damaged and another twenty-nine flyable but damaged. Midway's airfield was not put out of action and the bombers could still fly from there. The land defences were also barely damaged and at least one more aerial attack would be required before a seaborne invasion. The American bombers on the way to the Japanese carriers included six Grumman TBF Avengers, introducing the bombers to combat for the first time. This attack was repelled, and for the loss of two fighters, five of the six TBFs were destroyed, two SB2Us, eight SBDs and two B-26s were lost. One of the B-26s crashed close to the *Akagi* and it is perhaps this that led Admiral Nagumo to send his reserve force to Midway. The Japanese normally kept half their forces behind in case of attack and two squadrons each of dive and torpedo bombers were on the *Akagi* and *Kaga*. At 0715, they were rearmed with bombs for use against land targets. Twenty-five minutes later, an American force was spotted but the composition of this fleet was not noted. The bombers were quickly rearmed and Nagumo demanded to know the disposition of the American fleet, discovering it contained one carrier. The returning bombers and fighters were close by and would need to land immediately but Nagumo's reserve planes were not in position to take off. He couldn't do anything with his reserve. They were simply not ready. It was too late though! American bombers were on their way and had left the US carriers at 0700. Before it arrived, at 0753, another attack was made by land-based aircraft on the Japanese fleet.

With flights from *Enterprise* and *Hornet* on their way, *Yorktown*'s aircraft flew off at 0800. The Americans had literally just thrown their aircraft into the air, deeming that the force of attack was better than coordination of aircraft types and weapons. Basically, sinking the Japanese carriers was crucially important as only that could guarantee the safety of their own carriers. The uncoordinated attacks would lead to higher American casualties but Japanese tactics preferred coordinated attacks and the American thinking was that the constant attacks would prevent the Japanese flying off, thereby catching them with their pants down.

All of *Hornet*'s aircraft flew on the wrong course and most missed the Japanese carriers, with one squadron breaking off and flying on the correct course. Ten F4Fs ditched after running out of fuel. The squadron of torpedo bombers from *Hornet* began attacking at 0920, with another squadron from *Enterprise* arriving at 0930. Their fighter support ran low on fuel and turned back at 0940. All fifteen TBD Devastators from *Hornet* were shot down, as were ten of fourteen Devastators of *Enterprise*'s VT-6 and ten of twelve Devastators from *Yorktown* were shot down. It would be the last time the Devastator would be used in combat. Many had got close but their torpedoes were faulty and did not go off or missed completely. The close hits did see the Japanese carriers take severe evasive action. The Devastators, while failures on the attack, kept the Japanese from launching their counter-attack and caused some of the Zero combat air patrols to run out of fuel and ammunition.

At 1000, another attack on the Japanese carriers took place by aircraft from *Yorktown*. The Japanese combat air patrol quickly flew off to attack the bombers. Unfortunately for the Japanese, three squadrons of SBDs from *Enterprise* and *Yorktown* were coming in from the south-west and north-east. *Enterprise*'s two squadrons were low on fuel after ages spent searching for the enemy. It was the decision of squadron commander Wade McClusky that actually decided the fate

Above: The Japanese carrier *Hiryū* burns on 5 June. She was the last of four Japanese carriers lost during the battle. It was the end of Japan's domination of the Pacific.

of the whole Battle of Midway. He knew his aircraft would have to ditch after running out of fuel but the risk was worth it. He had spotted the destroyer *Arashi*, followed it back towards the main carrier force and, despite losing some bombers to fuel exhaustion even before the attack began, set course for the carriers. All three bomber squadrons miraculously arrived simultaneously, and with the Japanese fighters busy with the previous attackers, each of the three squadrons was just in the perfect position to coordinate attacks on the carriers. The Japanese carriers were refuelling and rearming, with fuel lines and ordnance scattered throughout the hangers and flight decks. They were at their most vulnerable. At 1022, *Enterprise*'s two squadrons split up to dive on both *Akagi* and *Kaga*, but both headed for *Kaga*. Some of the dive-bombers pulled out and changed course for *Akagi* but almost two full squadrons attacked *Kaga* and inflicted four or five direct hits, starting numerous fires and causing damage to the flight deck. One bomb, blowing up near the bridge, killed the captain and senior officers.

Within minutes *Akagi* was under attack, with the aircraft that diverted from *Kaga* diving on it. Only one bomb hit *Akagi* but it was a direct hit on the midship elevator. It exploded in the upper hangar deck, destroying the armed and fuelled aircraft. A near miss at the stern destroyed the rudder and bent the flight deck upwards. The first bomb and the resultant explosions had done their work. *Akagi* was doomed. *Yorktown*'s VB-3 squadron dropped onto *Sōryū*, with the carrier taking three hits. VT-3 went for *Hiryū* but scored no hits. *Sōryū* and *Kaga* were ablaze from bow to stern within six minutes, a pall of smoke rising from their flight decks. Their crews, those who survived, abandoned ship. *Akagi*'s fires started slowly but began to burn more fiercely. They could not be put out and she too was abandoned.

The sole surviving carrier, *Hiryū*, sent eighteen dive-bombers and six fighters after the retreating American aircraft. They attacked the first carrier, *Yorktown*, which was hit by three bombs. Her boilers were extinguished, a hole was blown in her flight deck and many of her anti-aircraft guns were damaged or destroyed. Twelve Japanese dive-bombers and four fighters were lost in the attack, which put *Yorktown* out of action for around an hour. Her flight deck was planked over and several boilers relit, giving her a speed of 19 kt and capability to resume air operations once more. Just as the damage was repaired, *Hiryū*'s second wave of planes, ten torpedo bombers and six Zero fighters, sighted the repaired *Yorktown*. They assumed it was a different carrier, the first flight having supposedly left *Yorktown* for dead. *Yorktown* was hit by two torpedoes and developed a 26° list. Losing all power, she was put out of action and the command staff moved to the cruiser *Astoria*.

The Japanese thought they had put two carriers out of action, sinking both; in reality damaging *Yorktown* twice, but not sinking her. Thinking the Americans had a single carrier left, the Japanese decided to make one more strike. For them, they would have completed the work begun at Pearl Harbor and have knocked out the American Pacific Fleet's flat-tops. The war would be won!

Late in the afternoon, a patrolling reconnaissance aircraft from *Yorktown* spotted *Hiryū*. *Enterprise* launched a strike of dive-bombers that included ten 'refugees' from *Yorktown*. Either four or five bombs hit *Hiryū*, despite twelve Zeros acting as fighter defence, and she was soon ablaze and unable to operate. Hornet's aircraft attacked the escorts but made no hits. *Hiryū*'s crew were evacuated and the ship abandoned, with the escorts sailing off in an attempt to find the US carriers. *Hiryū* did not sink immediately. She was afloat for a few hours and was spotted next day by an aircraft from the escort carrier *Hōshō* but sank soon after. Her captain, Rear Admiral Yamaguchi, went down with his ship.

With darkness falling, the Americans and Japanese considered their options. *Yorktown* was abandoned, the American carriers closed on the Japanese so their pilots could return safely from their long-distance missions. Not wanting a night-time meeting with the Japanese surface fleet, the carriers eventually turned to the east and withdrew, turning back towards the enemy near to midnight. The Japanese under Yamamoto searched for the carriers, but due to them turning back could not find them. They eventually withdrew to the west.

On 5 June, the Americans failed to find the Japanese forces again. They narrowly failed to locate the Japanese fleet late in the day and could not hit a straggling Japanese destroyer. At 0215, the submarine *Tambor*, 100 miles from Midway, sent a message to Midway about four large ships that passed it by. The Americans, unsure if this was Yamamoto's main force, were furious at the submarine's commander. In reality this force was a cruiser group sent to rid Midway and not the main force. At 0255, the Japanese cruiser force was ordered to turn back. As they changed course, *Tambor* was spotted and, in the evasive manoeuvres, two of the cruisers collided. *Mogami* and *Mikuma* were both badly damaged, with the bow of *Mogami* taking the brunt of the collision. Both ships slowed and as dawn broke, *Tambor* realised the ships were Japanese. The captain of *Tambor* made an unsuccessful attack on the cruisers before reporting them as Japanese. On return to port Murphy was relieved of command and sent to a shore station for his failures, which could have seen the Japanese cruisers all destroyed.

The carriers and land-based aircraft from Midway spent the next two days picking off stragglers from the Japanese fleets. *Mikuma* was sunk by Douglas Dauntlesses but *Mogami* survived and returned to Japan for repair. Two destroyers were bombed and strafed too.

Yorktown was taken in tow but the Japanese submarine I-168 sent two torpedoes into the side of *Yorktown*. A third torpedo hit the destroyer *Hammann*, which broke in two and took eighty crew with her. *Yorktown* sank at 0500 on 7 June. She was the one major US casualty, but most of her crew lived to fight another day. The Japanese were less lucky. They lost some 3,057 highly skilled sailors and airmen. On the aircraft carriers 2,181 lost their lives, with the worst casualties on *Kaga* (811) and *Sōryū* (711). 700 died on *Mikuma*. Total American losses were 307 killed for the loss of one aircraft carrier and one destroyer, neither sunk by the main Japanese fleet or their aircraft. The Japanese had lost four carriers, one heavy cruiser and 248 aircraft.

With 150 aircraft destroyed, the Americans turned for home and the USS *Saratoga*, now repaired after a torpedo attack, which was bringing replacement aircraft. The Japanese battle report assumed the fleet had been found accidentally and the Japanese did not suspect their codes had been broken. They had failed to destroy the American carriers once again and now the industrial might of America was beginning to come into play. The ships, pilots and aircraft lost by the Japanese could not be replaced effectively. Midway, while barely six months into the conflict, was certainly the midway point of the whole Pacific War. The Japanese army and civilian population were not informed as to the failure of the attack on Midway. Wounded Japanese sailors, who returned on 14 June, were placed in isolation and the sheer scale of the defeat not communicated.

The Japanese captured three American aviators, who were all killed by being tied to water-filled kerosene cans and thrown overboard to drown after being interrogated.

Like most battles, it was the war of attrition that ground down the Japanese forces, and the effects of Coral Sea and Midway decimated their fleet. No longer would the Japanese navy be the power it once was. No longer would the Japanese airmen be so dominant. No longer would the dominant naval weapon be the battleship. Air warfare and the flat-top would be the dominant naval weapons, and Japan had just lost four of its carriers, all of its aircraft and all of its highly-trained airmen. It would take a few more months for the tide to turn fully but turn it would. Japan, though would never recover from the loss of these four vital floating airstrips. Japan's war was lost. Only the geography of the Japanese gains in the Pacific, and the desire to wipe out the Germans and Italians first, saw the Battle of the Pacific take so long to win.

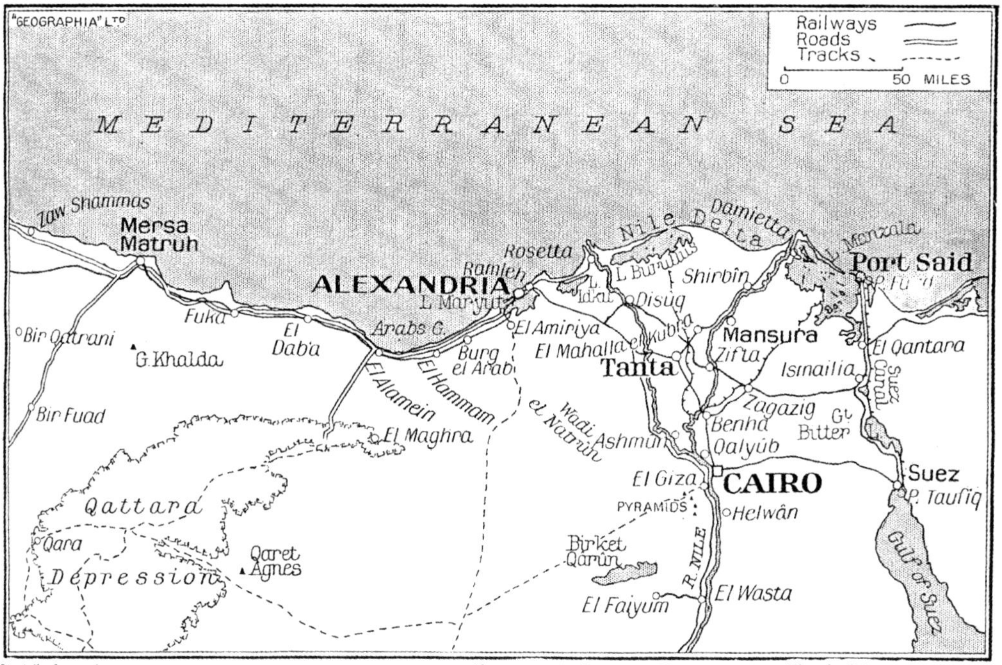

Specially drawn for Hutchinson's Pictorial History of the War by "Geographia" Ltd.

Above: Map of Egypt showing the coastal battleground where heavy fighting took place in June 1942. The German offensive saw Rommel's army passing El Daba to within about 90 miles from Alexandria.

Left: General Sir Claude Auchinleck, the British Commander-in-Chief, Middle East, consulting with a captain of the 50th Division in Egypt. On 21 June the German offensive forced the Allied forces to withdraw from the Tobruk garrison, resulting in the capture of about 30,000 men as well as essential fuel and other supplies. With Rommel still on the move, Auchinleck established a fortified line running for 40 miles inland from El Alamein down to the Qattara Depression in the south. This stabilised the front.

Above: Relief among a group of rescued New Zealand and British troops. *Below:* Corpses are strewn amid the wreckage of an ammunition train which has been attacked by British aircraft.

Above: This German wireless truck has been set alight by shellfire during a British 'nuisance' raid into enemy-held territory. *Below:* Naturally the British propaganda put a positive spin on Allied successes, and this photograph shows a knocked-out German tank being inspected.

Above: British anti-tank gun mounted on a lorry, with one of their kills, a German tank, in the background. *Below:* Cameraman of the Army Film & Photographic Unit during the fighting in Libya. The personnel of the AFPU were drawn from experienced photographers in the forces.

Although the Axis armies had forced the 8th Army back as far as El Alamein, local counter-attacks saw the capture of many groups of German and Italian soldiers, as shown above. *Below:* Field Marshal Erwin Rommel leads a column of vehicles into Tobruk. This British garrison had been unable to hold out until communications and supply lines could be re-established.

The Eastern Front

In February 1942 the Germans were in retreat on the Eastern Front, and these infantrymen are shown moving through the freezing fog, supported by tanks. Their summer offensive still saw major advances towards Stalingrad, but Hitler had awoken a sleeping bear and in November the Soviets launched a decisive counteroffensive at Stalingrad.

Above left: A German soldier runs during an engagement on the Eastern Front in the summer of 1942. He is holding a Mauser 98K carbine. *Above right:* A Messerschmitt Bf 110 acts as a spotter for the panzers, transmitting the position of the enemy's tanks. *Below:* The view from a Fieseler Storch reconnaissance aircraft looking down on a column of German troops.

As the conflict in the east continued, fuel was increasingly in short supply and every measure was taken to conserve it. *Above:* Luftwaffe ground crew use manpower to hoist a bomb into the belly of a Heinkel He 111. *Below:* Scavenging for fuel from Soviet railway tankers stranded by bombing raids on the railways.

Right: Air Chief Marshal Sir Arthur Travers Harris, christened by the press as 'Bomber Harris', was put in charge of RAF Bomber Command on 22 February 1942. *Below:* At Canterbury the Dean of the cathedral examines damage inflicted on the night of 31 May 1942, as part the 'Baedeker raids' in reprisal for the bombing of German cities.

Badges of Britain's Home Front Organisations

1. Women's Land Army, two years' service merit badge. 2. Merchant Navy, Civil Defence, Police, National Fire Service and other uniformed civilians; badge for brave conduct commendations. 3. Civil Defence, armlet worn by those responsible for investigating reports of unexploded bombs. 4. Civil Defence, qualified instructor. 5. Hospital Service, issued to all staff (except doctors and nurses) serving minimum of ninety-six hours a month. 6. Civil Defence, service badge, and 7, that worn by Incident Officers. 8. Civil Defence, Ambulance Driver and shoulder flash. 9. Workers in Royal Ordnance factories. 10. Boy Scouts war service armlet. 11. National Fire Service, cap badge. 12. Civil Defence, Post Warden and shoulder flash.

In 1942 women were taking over an increasing number of tasks to free the men up for other duties. *Above:* This Anti-Aircraft Command searchlight and sound locator unit is being entirely operated by members of the Auxiliary Territorial Service. By the end of the year there were sixty employments for women of the ATS, compared with only five in 1939.

Having proven themselves to be up to the task, ATS teams became a common sight operating barrage balloons from parks and areas of wasteland. *Above:* Dame Laura Knight's painting, 'A Balloon Site in Coventry'. *Below left:* A member of the ATS operating a balloon winch. *Below right:* Balloons were also flown from special tenders to protect the Thames Estuary.

The unsung heroes of the Home Front came in many guises.

Right: By the end of 1942 the output of Britain's steelworks and armament factories was reaching its targets, but the build-up of the fighting services had caused a manpower shortage that could only be solved by the substitution of women. This is Kathleen McCarthy, a former hairdresser, shown operating a machine for slotting the case striker body of a six-pounder gun at a Royal Ordnance factory.

Two portraits of the men of the Home Guard. *Left:* Sergeant Bluett of the Cornwall Home Guard. *Opposite page:* Company Sergeant Major Walters, of the Lancashire Home Guard.

In the Libyan desert a member of Rommel's Deutsches Afrika Korps (DAK) scans the horizon using a twin-lensed periscope, on the lookout for the British forces. Inevitably, living conditions in the searing heat of the desert were tough and the dust and heat took a heavy toll on vehicles, aircraft and other equipment.

Mixed Fortunes in North Africa
In the spring of 1942 Erwin Rommel, shown right, launched a major assault which saw the British forces driven back into Egypt as far as El Alamein, and Tobruk was also in German hands once again. But the Brits had a new field commander in the desert campaign, Bernard Law Montgomery, and by the end of the year his 'Desert Rats' had retaken El Alamein. It was the first major victory for the Allies and proved to be a turning point in the war.

Two paintings exhibited at the National Portrait Gallery, London, in the summer of 1943 and depicting action during the Battle of El Alamein. *Above:* 'Railway Station, Alamein', by Philip Bawcombe. *Below:* '25-Pounder Gun and Team in Action on the Alamein Front', by J. Berry.

Training for the Dieppe raid. Somewhere on the south coast of England these Royal Marines practise for the first landing operations on enemy-occupied territory. *Above:* A mock landing craft, waiting for the order to go ashore. *Below:* Scaling the cliffs after landing while under fire from live ammunition and ground charges.

These are the badges of twenty-five ships of the Royal Navy – battleships, cruisers, destroyers and submarines – just some of those that were lost on war service at sea during the year 1942. From the top: *Trinidad, Naiad, Barham, Neptune, Galatea, Edinburgh, Jaguar, Hermes, Jackal, Exeter, Somali, Olympus, Sikh, Eagle, Wild Swan, Bedouin, Kandahar, Hermione, Matabele, Vampire, Unbeaten, Triumph, Electra, Talisman* and *Thorn*.

Right: A boatswain of the Kriegsmarine summons the watch off duty to parade on the quarterdeck.

Below: German torpedo boats travelling at speed. They varied in size, but should not be confused with the smaller torpedo-armed Schnellboote, known by the Allies as E-boats.

Right: On the morning of 27 August 1942, the US battleship *Iowa* slid down the ways in Brooklyn Navy Yard into the East River. This photograph was taken shortly before, while the final preparations were being made. The first of a class of six, she had been laid down in June 1940. *Iowa* was 880 feet long overall, with a beam of 108 feet, and displaced 45,000 tons. Unofficially she was credited with a potential speed of 35 knots. Her main armament was nine 16-inch guns with a secondary armament of twenty 5-inch. Her sister ships were *New Jersey, Missouri, Wisconsin, Illinois* and *Kentucky.* USS *Iowa* also served in the Korean War and survives as a museum ship in the Pacific Battleship Center in Los Angeles.

Action on Guadalcanal

These paintings are by Lieutenant Dwight Shepler of the US Navy, an artist who served on the island during the fierce fighting of 1942–43. *Top:* 'Action on the River' shows Marines crossing a sluggish river. *Bottom:* 'Bombardment Guadalcanal' was painted during the 'first anniversary hate shoot' put down on 7 December 1942, one year after the Japanese attack on Pearl Harbor. The US Marine artillery fired 155-mm howitzers from dawn to dusk.

Right: A soldier surrenders to one of the small British patrols which were active in the desert.

Below: A British ambulance picks up a wounded infantryman. The vehicle is an Austin K2/Y heavy military ambulance. These were used extensively throughout the war and over 13,000 were built at the Austin Motor Company's plant at Longbridge. The K2/Y was based on the civilian K30 truck.

Air operations in the western desert. *Above:* Men of the Royal Australian Air Force (RAAF) are briefed by their squadron leader before a mission. The American-built Curtiss P-40 was a single-engine, all-metal, ground-attack aircraft that first flew in 1938. A modification of the P-36 Hawk, the Americans called it the Warhawk, the Brits Tomahawk and later variants were known as Kittyhawks. *Below:* Aircrew scramble when an enemy aircraft is spotted in the vicinity.

Above: The P-40 saw service with most Allied air forces and remained in frontline service until the end of the war. It first saw combat with the British Commonwealth Desert Air Force in Libya in 1941. No. 112 Squadron of the RAF was among the first to receive the Tomahawk and it was the first to apply the distinctive shark's teeth motiff, copying a design already seen on the Messerschmitt Bf 110.

Right: An Arab poses with ammunition belts while assisting in the reloading of an RAF Tomahawk.

Red Army soldiers concentrate their fire on enemy emplacements in an occupied village as Germany's summer offensive on the Eastern Front gathers momentum. By June the German 6th Army was driving towards Stalingrad.

Above left: Marshal Timoshenko was the Soviet Commander-in-Chief in the south-west, where the Red Army was fighting to keep the Germans out of the Caucasus oilfields. *Above right:* This crew of a light bomber have carried out their 200th operational mission in the defence of Leningrad. *Below:* With bayonets fixed, these Soviet troops pause to read letters from home.

Soviet tanks launching an attack along a sunken road in the Kharkov sector. For more on the T-34 tank see page 50.

Soviet infantry advancing. 'Using every available means of cover, the soldiers with automatic weapons, rifles and fixed bayonets make a cautious advance on a populated district.' Note the improvised observation post in the fork of a tree, shown on the left.

It was common practice among all armies to press serviceable captured enemy equipment into service. Shown above, Red Army troops make use of German tanks. These are Panzer III medium tanks, the most numerous of the German tanks of the Second World War, and some 5,774 were built by the time production ceased in 1945.

Middle right: Red Army Guards preparing a rubber pontoon for crossing a river. It is being inflated using a foot pump.

Bottom right: An American-supplied half-track is being used by the Russians as an artillery tractor to haul a field gun through in the rough and densely wooded terrain.

Cossacks and cavalry units continued to play an important part in the battles raging in the Caucasus. Shown above, a Russian cavalry unit is moving into position.

Infantrymen equipped with sub-machine guns edge forward under the protective cover provided by the T-34 tanks.

Overshadowed by events elsewhere, the Aleutian Islands Campaign, from 1 June 1942 to 15 August 1943, saw the US drive out a Japanese force which had occupied the islands of Attu and Kiska in the Alaskan territory. The Japanese were attempting to control the Pacific Great Circle routes, not as a way for them to invade the USA but to prevent the Americans from launching attacks across the north Pacific.

Top: The military base on the Aleutian Islands in Alaska. *Right:* This US propaganda poster is intended to reassure the American public that the Japanese could not invade via the Alaskan back door.

Having fled the German invasion in 1940, General Charles de Gaulle established and led the Free French movement – sometimes referred to as the 'Fighting French' by the British press at the time – rallying the overseas colonies and organising the resistance. He is shown here on two occasions in 1942. *Top:* Accompanied by Admiral Auboyneau, he visited French warships in British ports and is shown addressing the officers and men of the destroyer *Leopard*. *Bottom:* Inspecting men of the newly formed Fighting French commando unit at Wellington Barracks.

JULY 1942

Members of Leningrad's organised firefighting service on the lookout for fires. Just as in Britain, the Russian women carried out a wide range of wartime roles.

Top: First jet in the air, the single-engined He 178 flew in 1939 but failed to impress the RLM. *Middle:* The He 280 was Heinkel's rival to the Me 262, but its introduction was hampered by delays with the HeS 8 turbojet. *Below:* The Jumo 004, with the intake shown to the right.

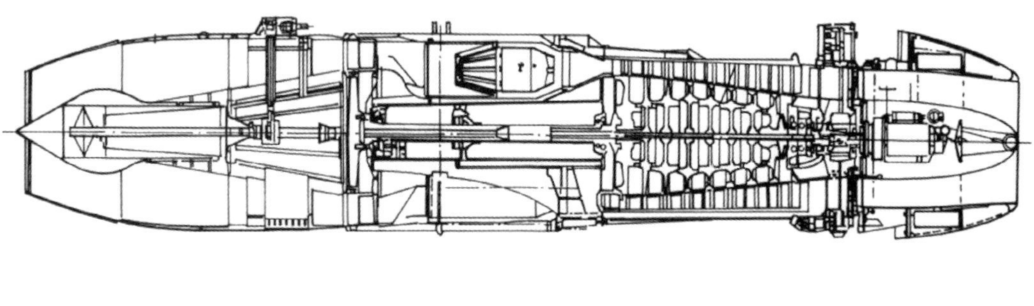

Genesis of the Jets

On 18 July 1942 the Messerschmitt Me 262 flew entirely under jet power for the first time from the airfield at Leipheim. Not the first turbojet to fly – that honour had gone to the Heinkel He 178 back in the summer of 1939 – it was the Me 262 that would become the world's first operational combat jet in late 1944.

Germany's interest in turbojets can be traced back to the early 1930s when Hans von Ohain began his research at the University of Göttingen. While von Ohain was aware of the British jet pioneer Frank Whittle, the two engineers are credited with developing their engines concurrently. By 1935 von Ohain had demonstrated the principle of his engine, and the following year he attracted the interest of the Heinkel company, for whom he produced the Heinkel-Hirth HeS 1 engine which featured a centrifugal compressor, annular combustion chamber and radial inflow turbine. This led to the development of the first flight engine, the HeS 3. Heinkel had been conducting this research of its own volition when, in 1938, the Reichluftfahrtminsterium instigated the parallel development of a suitable airframe and a jet engine with a view to creating an operational combat aircraft. Ironically, the Luftwaffe was enjoying considerable success with its piston-powered aircraft at that time, and the first demonstrations of the under powered He 178 failed to impress. It was only with the advent of the more powerful Jumo 004 and BMW 003 jet engines that the development of the Me 262 progressed to production. Equipped with the 004, as the 003 was not ready in time, it proved to be a revolutionary aircraft.

Below: The Me 262 prototype V3 prior to the first successful all-jet flight, 18 July 1942. This is a tail-dragger, with the third wheel at the rear. Production models sat on a tricycle undercarriage.

The arctic convoy PQ-13 bound for Russia with arms for the Soviet Army. *Above:* A crewman on one of the merchant ships attempts to clear away some of the accumulated ice. In the intense cold all metal objects could 'burn' to the naked touch. *Below:* Bringing up the rear of the convoy, stokers of a British cruiser are busy de-icing chains and capstans with a jet of steam.

Above: HMS *Howe* was the last of the King George V class of battleships and spent most of her wartime career on the Russian convoys. She was completed in August 1942 and decommissioned in 1950. She is shown with her distinctive camouflage.

Right: Officers and crew of HM Submarine *Tigris* which, with the *Trident*, inflicted severe losses on ships carrying reinforcements to German forces on the Murmansk front.

As the Germans made further gains towards Stalingrad, the Russians fled from the towns of Boguchar and Millerovo on 16 July. *Above:* German gunners keep watch for Red Army soldiers as the buildings burn. *Below:* Their adversary, a Russian soldier, hacking a trench in the Stalingrad sector.

Battle for the oilfields. *Right:* This map, showing the mineral resources, including oilfields, of the Caucasus, shows why the region was such a rich prize for the Germans. *Below:* When the Russians were forced to abandon an oilfield between Maykop and Krasnodar, they set the wells ablaze rather than have them fall into German hands.

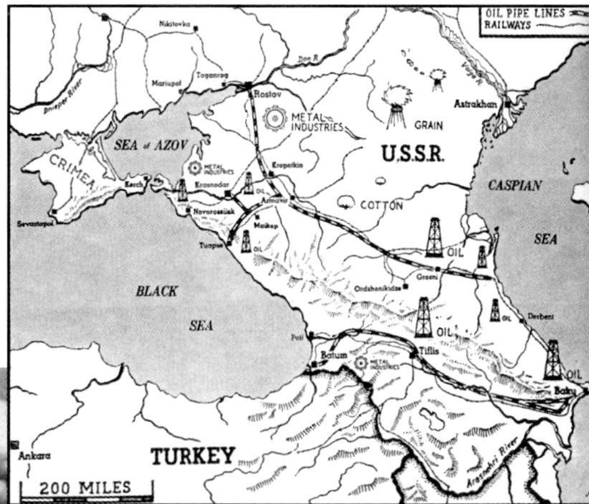

Infantrymen of the German 17th Army battle their way through Rostov-on-Don, which was heavily defended by the Russians. They took the harbour town on 23 July, thus opening the way into the Caucasus region of southern Russia with its important oilfields.

AUGUST 1942

Above: American soldiers board a troopship at Nouméa, bound for Guadalcanal. Nouméa is in New Caledonia in the south-west of the Pacific, and was the headquarters of the US military in the South Pacific.

When the Japanese invaded Guadalcanal in the Solomon Isalnds and began construction of an airfield at Lunga Point, it became imperative that the Allies retook the island. The initial landings by US Marines took place on 7 August 1942 and this was followed by six months of intensive fighting. *Above:* A Marine takes aim with a captured Nambu 6.5-mm light machine gun. *Below:* The crew pose in front of their American Light Tank M2, otherwise known as the Stuart.

Above: American wounded on Guadalcanal are treated before transfer to hospital. *Below:* Grave of a Japanese airman killed in June 1942. This was the first prolonged campaign in the Pacific and both sides suffered heavy losses, with around 7,100 US deaths and over 30,000 Japanese.

On 19 August 1942 a combined operations raid took place on the German-occupied port of Dieppe on the northern coast of France. The objective of Operation Rutter was to seize the port for a short time, to prove that it was possible, and to gather intelligence. But the raid was ill conceived and of the 6,068 infantrymen who made it ashore at Dieppe, predominantly Canadians, more than half were killed, wounded or captured. *Top:* The raid took place in daylight and this photograph shows the flotilla of light naval craft making its way across the Channel. *Middle:* Landing craft approaching the shore under the cover of a smokescreen. *Bottom:* They arrived off the French coast at 4.50 a.m. and troops were landed on six beaches.

Top right: RAF Film Unit photograph of Dieppe showing fires at the casino and at a tobacco factory which was used by the German military.

Middle right: Two tank landing craft alongside a British destroyer on their return from the Dieppe beaches. One of them contains a Bren carrier. In many ways Dieppe was a dress rehearsal for the big amphibious landings to come, a means of testing equipment and techniques. If any good came of the raid it was in pointing the way for the success of D-Day in 1944.

Bottom right: Some of the less seriously wounded men clamber aboard a destroyer while the land operations are still in progress.

Top: German photograph showing soldiers examining one of the invasion beaches after the assault of Dieppe. Note the abandoned tanks and equipment. *Bottom:* Some of the armoured vehicles did return from Dieppe and are shown landing on a British beach. Churchill described the raid as a 'reconnaissance force' and 'an indispensable preliminary to full-scale operations'.

Above: Some of the more seriously wounded are being brought aboard a destroyer after the action, while, on the right, this wounded soldier chats with a colleague on the quayside after making it back to England. *Below:* A German prisoner captured at Dieppe is being escorted off one of the British vessels. Note the Bren guns carried by three of the Allied troops and also the distinctive woollen headgear worn by the men on the raid.

Operation Pedestal saw three aircraft carriers escort a number of merchant ships to Malta, which was besieged by the Germans and Italians. The carriers carried spare aircraft for Malta, which would be flown off and sent to the island to bolster the defences there. In the bottom image, a bomb narrowly misses one of the merchant ships in the convoy.

Desperate efforts to prevent the passage of Allied convoys through the Mediterranean were made by Axis aircraft, but only a few vessels were lost. *Above:* These troops are going ashore at the Grand Harbour, Malta. *Below:* The civilian population of Malta became hardened to the repeated raids by enemy aircraft. These people are clearing away the earth and stones that were thrown up when a bomb fell on this street very close to the bus.

Right: British naval officer on a Lend-Lease destroyer on transatlantic convoy escort duties.

Below: Convoy guardians. The crew of a destroyer's .5 anti-aircraft gun at action stations ready to drive off attacking enemy aircraft.

Above: HM Submarine *Thunderbolt* returning to base after successful operations against enemy shipping. Like most British subs she carried the Jolly Roger, with symbols denoting the type of vessels she had attacked, including two U-boats and five supply ships sunk. *Below:* Lieutenant-Commander C. B. Crouch, captain of the *Thunderbolt,* shown grasping the ship's periscope.

Above: Inside the torpedo room of a British submarine, showing a 21-inch torpedo being loaded into the torpedo tube. The subs were active in the North Sea, Atlantic and Mediterranean. *Below:* The subs were fitted with Davis escape apparatus which is used when a the vessel cannot surface, and this crew member is demonstrating the escape route through the safety hatch.

Above: The crew of HM Submarine *Thrasher*, ready to go on leave after an eighteen-month stint in the Mediterranean where she is said to have sunk 40,000 tons of enemy shipping.

Right: The submariner's greatest fear was the depth charge. Here a depth charge explodes underwater, making the surface heave and throwing up a cascade of water. The gunner on this Coastal Forces motor gunboat is strapped to his gun.

Following a three-hour chase in the North Atlantic on 8 August 1942, the convoy-escort *Dianthus* forced U-379 to the surface through depth charges, and then rammed and sank her. The top photograph shows the damage done to the ship's hull. *Bottom:* Some of the prisoners from the U-boat disembarking from *Dianthus*. Rammed four times, the bows of the U-boat reared up to smash against the side of the corvette's deck.

SEPTEMBER 1942

The Boeing B-29 Superfortress first took to the skies on 21 September 1942. When it was introduced into service two years later it became one of the largest aircraft to see action in the Second World War. This high-altitude strategic bomber was a very advanced aircraft for its time with a pressurised cabin, electronic fire-control systems, and remote-controlled gun turrets.

The Wannsee Protocol

TOP SECRET – 30 copies

Minutes of discussion.

I. The following persons took part in the discussion about the final solution of the Jewish question, which took place in Berlin, am Grossen Wannsee No. 56/58, on 20 January 1942:

- Dr Alfred Meyer, State Secretary (Staatssekretär) Reich Ministry for the Occupied Eastern Territories
- Erich Neumann, State Secretary (Staatssekretär) Office of the Plenipotentiary for the Four-Year Plan
- Dr Josef Bühler, State Secretary (Staatssekretär) Government of the Governor General in Cracow
- Dr Gerhard Klopfer, Nazi Party Chancellery Permanent Secretary (Ministerialdirektor)
- Adolf Eichmann, Reich Security Main Office Director of Section IV B 4
- Dr Rudolf Lange, Commander of the Security Police and Security Service (KdS)
- Martin Luther, Undersecretary of State (Unterstaatssekretär) German Foreign Office
- Dr Georg Leibbrandt, Reich Ministry for the Occupied Eastern Territories Permanent Secretary (Ministerialdirektor)
- Dr Wilhelm Stuckart, State Secretary (Staatssekretär) Reich Ministry of the Interior
- Dr Roland Freisler, State Secretary (Staatssekretär) Reich Ministry of Justice
- Reinhard Heydrich, Head of the Security Police and Security Service (SD) Deputy Reich Protector of Bohemia and Moravia
- Wilhelm Kritzinger, Reich Chancellery Permanent Secretary (Ministerialdirektor)
- Otto Hofmann, Head of the SS Race and Settlement Main Office
- Dr Eberhard Schöngarth, Commander in Chief of Security Police and Security Service (BdS)
- Heinrich Müller, Reich Security Main Office Head of Department (Amt) IV

II. At the beginning of the discussion Chief of the Security Police and of the SD, SS-Obergruppenführer Heydrich, reported that the Reich Marshal had appointed him delegate for the preparations for the final solution of the Jewish question in Europe and pointed out that this discussion had been called for the purpose of clarifying fundamental questions. The wish of the Reich Marshal to have a draft sent to him concerning organisational, factual and material interests in relation to the final solution of the Jewish question in Europe makes necessary an initial common action of all central offices immediately concerned with these questions, in order to bring their general activities into line. The Reichsführer-SS and the Chief of the German Police (Chief of the Security Police and the SD) was entrusted with the official central handling of the final solution of the Jewish question without regard to geographic borders. The Chief of the Security Police and the SD then gave a short report of the struggle which has been carried on thus far against this enemy, the essential points being the following:

a) the expulsion of the Jews from every sphere of life of the German people,
b) the expulsion of the Jews from the living space of the German people.

In carrying out these efforts, an increased and planned acceleration of the emigration of the Jews from Reich territory was started, as the only possible present solution.

By order of the Reich Marshal, a Reich Central Office for Jewish Emigration was set up in January 1939 and the Chief of the Security Police and SD was entrusted with the management. Its most important tasks were

a) to make all necessary arrangements for the preparation for an increased emigration of the Jews,
b) to direct the flow of emigration,
c) to speed the procedure of emigration in each individual case.

The aim of all this was to cleanse German living space of Jews in a legal manner.

All the offices realised the drawbacks of such enforced accelerated emigration. For the time being they had, however, tolerated it on account of the lack of other possible solutions of the problem.

The work concerned with emigration was, later on, not only a German problem, but also a problem with which the authorities of the countries to which the flow of emigrants was being directed would have to deal. Financial difficulties, such as the demand by various foreign governments for increasing sums of money to be presented at the time of the landing, the lack of shipping space, increasing restriction of entry permits, or the cancelling of such, increased extraordinarily the difficulties of emigration. In spite of these difficulties, 537,000 Jews were sent out of the country between the takeover of power and the deadline of 31 October 1941. Of these

approximately 360,000 were in Germany proper on 30 January 1933
approximately 147,000 were in Austria (Ostmark) on 15 March 1939
approximately 30,000 were in the Protectorate of Bohemia and Moravia on 15 March 1939.

The Jews themselves, or their Jewish political organisations, financed the emigration. In order to avoid impoverished Jews remaining behind, the principle was followed that wealthy Jews have to finance the emigration of poor Jews; this was arranged by imposing a suitable tax, i.e. an emigration tax, which was used for financial arrangements in connection with the emigration of poor Jews and was imposed according to income.

Apart from the necessary Reichsmark exchange, foreign currency had to be presented at the time of landing. In order to save foreign exchange held by Germany, the foreign Jewish financial organisations were – with the help of Jewish organisations in Germany – made responsible for arranging an adequate amount of foreign currency. Up to 30 October 1941, these foreign Jews donated a total of around 9,500,000 dollars.

In the meantime the Reichsführer-SS and Chief of the German Police had prohibited emigration of Jews due to the dangers of an emigration in wartime and due to the possibilities of the east.

III. Another possible solution of the problem has now taken the place of emigration, i.e. the evacuation of the Jews to the East, provided that the Führer gives the appropriate approval in advance.

These actions are, however, only to be considered provisional, but practical experience is already being collected which is of the greatest importance in relation to the future final solution of the Jewish question.

Approximately 11 million Jews will be involved in the final solution of the European Jewish question, distributed as follows among the individual countries:

Country/Number

A.
Germany proper 131,800
Austria 43,700
Eastern territories 420,000
General Government 2,284,000
Bialystok 400,000
Protectorate Bohemia and Moravia 74,200
Estonia – free of Jews
Latvia 3,500
Lithuania 34,000
Belgium 43,000
Denmark 5,600
France, occupied territory 165,000
unoccupied territory 700,000
Greece 69,600
Netherlands 160,800
Norway 1,300

B.
Bulgaria 48,000
England 330,000
Finland 2,300
Ireland 4,000
Italy including Sardinia 58,000
Albania 200
Croatia 40,000
Portugal 3,000
Rumania including Bessarabia 342,000
Sweden 8,000
Switzerland 18,000
Serbia 10,000
Slovakia 88,000
Spain 6,000
Turkey (European portion) 55,500
Hungary 742,800
USSR 5,000,000
Ukraine 2,994,684
White Russia excluding Bialystok 446,484

Total over 11,000,000

The number of Jews given here for foreign countries includes, however, only those Jews who still adhere to the Jewish faith, since some countries still do not have a definition of the term 'Jew' according to racial principles.

The handling of the problem in the individual countries will meet with difficulties due to the attitude and outlook of the people there, especially in Hungary and Rumania. Thus, for example, even today the Jew can buy documents in Rumania that will officially prove his foreign citizenship.

The influence of the Jews in all walks of life in the USSR is well known. Approximately 5 million Jews live in the European part of the USSR, in the Asian part scarcely ¼ million.

The breakdown of Jews residing in the European part of the USSR according to trades was approximately as follows:

Agriculture 9.1 %
Urban workers 14.8 %
In trade 20.0 %
Employed by the state 23.4 %
In private occupations such as medical profession, press, theatre, etc. 32.7%

Under proper guidance, in the course of the final solution the Jews are to be allocated for appropriate labour in the East. Able-bodied Jews, separated according to sex, will be taken in large work columns to these areas for work on roads, in the course of which action doubtless a large portion will be eliminated by natural causes.

The possible final remnant will, since it will undoubtedly consist of the most resistant portion, have to be treated accordingly, because it is the product of natural

Below: Hungarian Jews are herded to the trains that will take them to Auschwitz.

Above: The boys and girls in the 'striped pyjamas' of a concentration camp.

selection and would, if released, act as a the seed of a new Jewish revival (see the experience of history).

In the course of the practical execution of the final solution, Europe will be combed through from west to east. Germany proper, including the Protectorate of Bohemia and Moravia, will have to be handled first due to the housing problem and additional social and political necessities.

The evacuated Jews will first be sent, group by group, to so-called transit ghettos, from which they will be transported to the east.

SS-Obergruppenführer Heydrich went on to say that an important prerequisite for the evacuation as such is the exact definition of the persons involved.

It is not intended to evacuate Jews over sixty-five years old, but to send them to an old-age ghetto – Theresienstadt is being considered for this purpose.

In addition to these age groups – of the approximately 280,000 Jews in Germany proper and Austria on 31 October 1941, approximately 3 per cent are over sixty-five years old – severely wounded veterans and Jews with war decorations (Iron Cross I) will be accepted in the old-age ghettos. With this expedient solution, in one fell swoop many interventions will be prevented.

The beginning of the individual larger evacuation actions will largely depend on military developments. Regarding the handling of the final solution in those European countries occupied and influenced by us, it was proposed that the appropriate expert of the Foreign Office discuss the matter with the responsible official of the Security Police and SD.

In Slovakia and Croatia the matter is no longer so difficult, since the most substantial problems in this respect have already been brought near a solution. In Rumania the government has in the meantime also appointed a commissioner for Jewish affairs. In order to settle the question in Hungary, it will soon be necessary to force an adviser for Jewish questions onto the Hungarian government.

With regard to taking up preparations for dealing with the problem in Italy, SS-Obergruppenführer Heydrich considers it opportune to contact the chief of police with a view to these problems.

In occupied and unoccupied France, the registration of Jews for evacuation will in all probability proceed without great difficulty.

Under Secretary of State Luther calls attention in this matter to the fact that in some countries, such as the Scandinavian states, difficulties will arise if this problem is dealt with thoroughly and that it will therefore be advisable to defer actions in these countries. Besides, in view of the small numbers of Jews affected, this deferral will not cause any substantial limitation.

The Foreign Office sees no great difficulties for south-east and western Europe.

SS-Gruppenführer Hofmann plans to send an expert to Hungary from the Race and Settlement Main Office for general orientation at the time when the Chief of the Security Police and SD takes up the matter there. It was decided to assign this expert from the Race and Settlement Main Office, who will not work actively, as an assistant to the police attaché.

IV. In the course of the final solution plans, the Nuremberg Laws should provide a certain foundation, in which a prerequisite for the absolute solution of the problem is also the solution to the problem of mixed marriages and persons of mixed blood.

The Chief of the Security Police and the SD discusses the following points, at first theoretically, in regard to a letter from the chief of the Reich chancellery:

1) Treatment of Persons of Mixed Blood of the First Degree
Persons of mixed blood of the first degree will, as regards the final solution of the Jewish question, be treated as Jews. From this treatment the following exceptions will be made:

a) Persons of mixed blood of the first degree married to persons of German blood if their marriage has resulted in children (persons of mixed blood of the second degree). These persons of mixed blood of the second degree are to be treated essentially as Germans.
b) Persons of mixed blood of the first degree, for whom the highest offices of the Party and State have already issued exemption permits in any sphere of life. Each individual case must be examined, and it is not ruled out that the decision may be made to the detriment of the person of mixed blood.

The prerequisite for any exemption must always be the personal merit of the person of mixed blood. (Not the merit of the parent or spouse of German blood.)

Persons of mixed blood of the first degree who are exempted from evacuation will be sterilised in order to prevent any offspring and to eliminate the problem of persons of mixed blood once and for all. Such sterilisation will be voluntary. But it is required to remain in the Reich. The sterilised 'person of mixed blood' is thereafter free of all restrictions to which he was previously subjected.

2) Treatment of Persons of Mixed Blood of the Second Degree
Persons of mixed blood of the second degree will be treated fundamentally as persons of German blood, with the exception of the following cases, in which the persons of mixed blood of the second degree will be considered as Jews:

a) The person of mixed blood of the second degree was born of a marriage in which both parents are persons of mixed blood.
b) The person of mixed blood of the second degree has a racially especially undesirable appearance that marks him outwardly as a Jew.
c) The person of mixed blood of the second degree has a particularly bad police and political record that shows that he feels and behaves like a Jew.

Also in these cases exemptions should not be made if the person of mixed blood of the second degree has married a person of German blood.

3) Marriages Between Full Jews and Persons of German Blood
Here it must be decided from case to case whether the Jewish partner will be evacuated or whether, with regard to the effects of such a step on the German relatives, [this mixed marriage] should be sent to an old-age ghetto.

4) Marriages Between Persons of Mixed Blood of the First Degree and Persons of German Blood

a) Without Children.
If no children have resulted from the marriage, the person of mixed blood of the first degree will be evacuated or sent to an old-age ghetto (same treatment as in the case of marriages between full Jews and persons of German blood, point 3).

b) With Children.
If children have resulted from the marriage (persons of mixed blood of the second degree), they will, if they are to be treated as Jews, be evacuated or sent to a ghetto along with the parent of mixed blood of the first degree. If these children are to be treated as Germans (regular cases), they are exempted from evacuation as is therefore the parent of mixed blood of the first degree.

5) Marriages between Persons of Mixed Blood of the First Degree and Persons of Mixed Blood of the First Degree or Jews.
In these marriages (including the children) all members of the family will be treated as Jews and therefore be evacuated or sent to an old-age ghetto.

6) Marriages Between Persons of Mixed Blood of the First Degree and Persons of Mixed Blood of the Second Degree.
In these marriages both partners will be evacuated or sent to an old-age ghetto without consideration of whether the marriage has produced children, since

possible children will as a rule have stronger Jewish blood than the Jewish person of mixed blood of the second degree.

SS-Gruppenführer Hofmann advocates the opinion that sterilisation will have to be widely used, since the person of mixed blood who is given the choice whether he will be evacuated or sterilised would rather undergo sterilisation.

State Secretary Dr. Stuckart maintains that carrying out in practice of the just mentioned possibilities for solving the problem of mixed marriages and persons of mixed blood will create endless administrative work. In the second place, as the biological facts cannot be disregarded in any case, State Secretary Dr Stuckart proposed proceeding to forced sterilisation.

Furthermore, to simplify the problem of mixed marriages possibilities must be considered with the goal of the legislator saying something like: 'These marriages have been dissolved.'

With regard to the issue of the effect of the evacuation of Jews on the economy, State Secretary Neumann stated that Jews who are working in industries vital to the war effort, provided that no replacements are available, cannot be evacuated.

SS-Obergruppenführer Heydrich indicated that these Jews would not be evacuated according to the rules he had approved for carrying out the evacuations then underway.

State Secretary Dr Bühler stated that the General Government would welcome it if the final solution of this problem could be begun in the General Government, since on the one hand transportation does not play such a large role here nor would problems of labour supply hamper this action. Jews must be removed from the territory of the General Government as quickly as possible, since it is especially here that the Jew as an epidemic carrier represents an extreme danger and on the other hand he is causing permanent chaos in the economic structure of the country through continued black market dealings. Moreover, of the approximately 2½ million Jews concerned, the majority is unfit for work.

State Secretary Dr Bühler stated further that the solution to the Jewish question in the General Government is the responsibility of the Chief of the Security Police and the SD and that his efforts would be supported by the officials of the General Government. He had only one request, to solve the Jewish question in this area as quickly as possible.

In conclusion the different types of possible solutions were discussed, during which discussion both Gauleiter Dr Meyer and State Secretary Dr Bühler took the position that certain preparatory activities for the final solution should be carried out immediately in the territories in question, in which process alarming the populace must be avoided.

The meeting was closed with the request of the Chief of the Security Police and the SD to the participants that they afford him appropriate support during the carrying out of the tasks involved in the solution.

Above: Men of HMS *Warspite* during a practice attack by aircraft from the carrier HMS *Formidable*. *Below: Warspite* with *Formidable* in the background. This crewman is on duty at a pom-pom gun and is seated in the 'Snotty's Chair', so named because it was introduced by a midshipman. In September the ship covered the landing at Mahajanga and Tamatave during the Allied invasion of the Vichy-controlled island of Madagascar in the Indian Ocean theatre.

Right: Hoisting shells aboard HMS *Warspite* for her eight 15-inch guns. In addition to these heavy-cailibre guns, she also had eight 6-inch, eight 4-inch long-range anti-aircraft guns and twenty-four smaller guns. The *Warspite* was also fitted with a catapult and carried four aircraft.

Below: Local Tamil crew prepare a Catalina flying boat carrying out Indian Ocean patrols from Ceylon (now known as Sri Lanka).

Above: This Sunderland flyingboat made a forced landing 4 miles off the Cyrenaiean coast after being attacked by a pair of Messerschmitts. Fortunately it remained afloat for two and a half hours by which time the crew were able to swim ashore. In the lower photograph the Sunderland is starting to break up.

OCTOBER 1942

A sign of the Allied successes in North Africa as the retaken Axis highway, the Strada dell'Asse, is renamed as Democracy Lane.

The Battle of El Alamein starts well for the Allies on 23 October 1943 with Montgomery's armour pushing into gaps cleared of enemy mines. *Above left:* An Australian infantryman attacks enemy vehicles using a 2-lb mortar. *Above right:* New Zealanders firing at Stuka dive-bombers. *Below:* A captured German 3.7-cm Pak anti-tank gun is turned on its former owners.

Above: General Alexander, who replaced Auchinleck as the Commander-in-Chief, Middle East, in August 1942, is shown crossing the airfield upon arrival in Egypt.

Top right: A British supply convoy almost receives a direct hit from an enemy bomb.

Middle right: Well armoured, this American-built M3 half-track has been equipped with a 75-mm howitzer as a tank-destroyer.

Bottom right: Tank transporters carry reconditioned Crusaders to the battle line. The tank transporters save wear and tear of the tanks' engines and tracks when being moved over longer distance.

As the war progressed women were to take over more of the roles previously carried out by men. This included 'manning' the barrage balloons that protected London and a number of other cities and towns, as well as important sites such as harbours and major bridges. Looking after and operating the balloons seven days a week, in all weathers and sometimes under bombardment, was an arduous task. But the women, often living on site in more remote locations, proved to be more than up to it, to the extent that the Ministry of Information announced that 'the substitution of WAAF for airmen on balloon sites does not imply that the airmen have in any sense been doing a woman's job'. *Above: Picture Post* cover of a balloon girl, June 1942.

Above: The WAAFs were shown the ropes at a training school at Cardington, Bedfordshire, where the former airship hangars that once housed the R101 and R100 were crammed tight with silvery barrage balloons. *Right:* The novelty of the situation attracted the advertisers. One for Weetabix had the headline, 'Keep War Workers Fighting Fit. On a Man's Job – and Equal to It.'

The raids continue. *Above:* Rescue teams and soldiers search the debris of houses wrecked by daylight raids on London and several other towns on 19 October 1942. *Below:* Boston bombers of the USAAF attack Le Havre docks, also in daylight and also in October.

NOVEMBER/DECEMBER 1942

US troops rest on the harbourside at Fédala, in Morocco, following the Operation Torch invasion of French North Africa. This had commenced on 8 November 1942.

Operation Torch

On 8 November 1942, the British-American invasion of French North Africa began. A Second Front was required to relieve the pressure on the Russians, who were being attacked by the Axis forces. Stalin had demanded action and Torch was the result. The Americans had wanted a frontal attack on Europe but Churchill was wary of this and Torch was the outcome. Torch would help remove the Germans and Italians from North Africa, securing the Mediterranean and providing a jumping off point for an attack on the soft underbelly of occupied Europe.

The plan was to attack Morocco, Algeria and Tunisia, held by the Vichy French. There were 125,000 French soldiers in the colonies, with 2,310 tanks and 500 aircraft. At Casablanca were ten warships and eleven submarines. Allied thinking was that the Vichy French would capitulate quickly and not shoot at the Americans. However, British ships had tried to sink many of the French fleet at Mers-él-Kebir in 1940 and it was assumed the French may fight the British as a result. Gibraltar was chosen as the headquarters of Operation Torch, with Eisenhower in overall control and Admiral Sir Andrew Cunningham providing leadership of the naval forces. Vice-Admiral Sir Bertram Ramsay would plan the amphibious landings, which would give the Allies an opportunity to test out their plans and equipment for invasion of northern Europe while not being under so much fire.

Oran, Algiers and Casablanca would be the original key targets, with a landing in Tunis to prevent supplies reaching Rommel's Afrika Korps in Libya. The plan was modified, though, as Tunis was too close to Luftwaffe bases in Sicily and Sardinia. The Allies were only capable of making three amphibious landings and the plans were modified to see landings at Casablanca, Oran and Algiers. The Americans tried to determine the French reaction to the effects of an invasion and used men based at their consulate in Algeria to find out. The results were positive. Invasion and capture of the ports and airfields would be followed by an advance to Tunisia, along with a pincer movement from Libya to force the Axis forces out of Africa.

Units attacking Casablanca were all American, with 35,000 troops of the 2nd Armored Division, and the 3rd and 9th Infantry Divisions, transported in around 100 ships. These men came direct from the USA rather than via Britain. In the centre, attacking Oran, were the US 509th Parachute Infantry Regiment, the US 1st Infantry Division and the US 1st Armored Division, comprising 18,500 troops, who sailed from Britain. Aimed at Algiers was the Eastern Task Force, with brigades of the British 78th and US 34th Infantry Divisions. Also included in the attack were two Commando units (No. 1 and No. 6). In total, 20,000 troops faced Algiers. The British troops all wore American uniforms. A convoy of ships headed for Britain was used to divert U-boats away from the invasion forces. Air cover was provided by British and US aircraft, using Gibraltar and aircraft carriers.

Opposite, inset: Paratroops disembarking at Algiers, and US troops in a landing craft. *Main image:* Grumman and Douglas aircraft on a carrier, heading for the Torch landings in North Africa.

Just before daybreak on 8 November, the Western task force landed near Casablanca. It was thought the French would not attack back and no preliminary bombardment took place. It was a mistake as many American troops died during the landings. A coup had been attempted the night before by forces who wanted to surrender to the Allies, but it was rebuffed and the forces alerted. When the French guns opened fire, the US ships offshore began to bombard the defences. Despite the defenders' attempts, by 10 November Casablanca had capitulated. French naval casualties included a cruiser, six destroyers and six submarines, destroyed by gunfire and aircraft. Two American destroyers were damaged.

Planning for the attack at Oran included the delivery of 116 Spitfires in cases that were sent to Gibraltar by sea and assembled in just eleven days. Three beaches were used for the invasion, one east and two west of the city. Landings in the west were delayed after a French convoy passed as the mines were being cleared. Damage was also caused to landing ships due to the shallowness of the beaches. It was a valuable lesson learned and pre-invasion reconnaissance was a major part of the D-Day landings in 1944. The French fleet in Oran attacked but were all sunk. Heavy fighting took place in and around Oran but the bombardment by British battleships on 9 November saw the city surrender.

Operation Torch saw the first major US airborne attack, with the US 509th Parachute Infantry Regiment flying from the UK. Poor weather over Spain and the range caused huge problems and thirty of the thirty-seven aircraft were forced to land in a dry salt lake west of the airfields of Tafraoui and La Sénia.

At Algiers, a coup took place in the early hours of 8 November. Some 400 resistance fighters seized the telephone exchange, radio station and the headquarters of the French 19th Corps. The fighters could not convince the French commander

Below: A merchant ship sunk during the Allied raid on the French fleet at Casablanca.

Above: An Italian-German commission was negotiating with the French in Morocco when US troops landed in North Africa. They were captured and marched away under guard.

to surrender to the Allies, and he was set free by gendarmes later in the morning. The invasion itself took place over three beaches, two west and one east of Algiers. The resistance had silenced the guns along the shore and the landings were made almost unopposed. One French officer openly welcomed the Allies. Only in Algiers itself was there any notable resistance. Two British destroyers had entered the port to land US Rangers onto the dockside. Both were driven back, but not after 250 Rangers had been disembarked from one of them. The city surrendered at 1800.

In a strange coincidence, French Admiral Darian was in Algiers on a private visit and the Allies offered him command of the French forces in North Africa in return for the surrender of the colonies. Hitler immediately ordered the invasion of Vichy France. At the same time, German forces were sent to bolster the Afrika Korps in Tunisia. The French forces in North Africa remained the same, with no place for the Free French. In Tunisia, the weak French forces made no effort to stop the German invasion. Charles de Gaulle, leader of the Free French, was furious but the Allies had no option if they wanted to secure North Africa quickly and attack the Germans in Tunisia and Libya. With the gradual integration of the Vichy forces in North Africa into the Allied war effort, Vichy colonies in West Africa joined the Allies too.

The results of the invasion itself included the occupation by the Germans of Vichy France, as well as the attempted capture and subsequent scuttling of the French fleet at Toulon. The campaign in North Africa was completed by May, with the surrender of the Axis forces, paving the way for the invasion of Europe proper, and the first stage attack on Sicily.

Above: The Vichy French ships burn in the harbour at Toulon following the scuttling of the fleet to keep it out of German hands. *Below:* Flames billow from one of the battleships. A few vessels escaped to North Africa, but most were slowly salvaged during and after the war.

Scuttling of the Vichy French Fleet at Toulon

Not since the sinking of the German High Seas Fleet at Scapa Flow, in 1919 had there been such a sight. In November 1942, over seventy vessels were scuttled by the French navy to prevent their capture by the Germans and Italians. It was the end of the French pre-war navy as it had already seen many ships lost in battles with the British at Mers-el-Kébir and Dakar in 1940 – actions between allies to prevent the use of the ships by the Germans – and the one thing that had been promised by the French Admiral Darlan would never happen.

It was an amazingly quick series of events that led to the scuttling of three battleships, seven cruisers, fifteen destroyers, twelve submarines and numerous other small vessels with the loss of twelve lives and twenty-six wounded. The invasion of North Africa by the Allies had been the catalyst for the invasion by the Germans of Vichy France, and the danger of the French fleet defecting to the Allies was too great for the Axis countries to allow it to remain in French hands.

The Germans had planned for the takeover of the fleet in Toulon almost since the creation of Vichy France but it was the discovery that Admiral François Darlan, commander of the Vichy navy, had been secretly offered the control of French North Africa if he defected to the Allied cause that spurred the Germans into action. With the invasion of North Africa on the 8th, Hitler ordered Case Anton to be put into action. By 10 November, German and Italian forces were in place to begin the invasion of the remainder of France. The Italians invaded the French Riviera and Corsica, while German tanks reached the Mediterranean coast by the next night. The 50,000-strong Vichy French army took up positions surrounding Toulon but were no match for the battle-hardened Germans. The German High Command planned Operation Lila, the capture of the French fleet intact, which would help change the balance of sea power in the Mediterranean, as well as providing Germany with a fully equipped naval base in the Western Mediterranean, providing a means of preventing Allied convoys heading for Malta and to the North African Mediterranean ports, should they be captured by the Allies.

On 19 November, Operation Lila was triggered, with a date of 27 November for the attack. German forces had been surrounding Toulon since the 11th and Admiral Auphan, Secretary of the Navy, had already ordered that the Vichy forces were to oppose the entry of the Axis troops into the navy establishments, or aboard the Vichy ships, and if the former proved impossible to scuttle the vessels. The original plan was to capsize the vessels but orders were changed so that the ships could be sunk on an even keel to enable recovery after the war had ended.

At 4 a.m. on 27 November, German forces entered Toulon, meeting sporadic opposition and quickly capturing Fort Lamalgue and Mourillon arsenal, as well as the main arsenal and the coastal defences of the port. Despite the speed of the capture of Admiral Marquis, his chief of staff managed to telephone to the chief of the arsenal, Contre Admiral Dornon, who transmitted the order to scuttle the ships and to fire on any troops approaching the vessels. Within twenty minutes the submarines were under attack, but many were already being scuttled. Some were moved to deeper water, while under fire, to scuttle where they would be harder to recover. The captain of the sub *Casablanca* dived his vessel at 5.40 a.m. and sailed for Algiers. Unfortunately for the main force of Germans, the maze of routes around the naval base saw them get lost and they were almost an hour behind schedule as they approached the main gates. The sentries engaged them and demanded to see paperwork before letting them through, again delaying them without firing a shot. This gave the ships time to prepare their charges and to be ready to open seacocks. The battleship *Strasbourg*, the pride of the French fleet and its most modern vessel, ordered the fleet to scuttle as the German tanks rolled into the base. By radio, flag and dispatch boat, the signal to 'Scuttle, Scuttle, Scuttle' soon reached every ship of the fleet and seacocks were opened, letting water flood into the ships from the mighty battleship *Strasbourg* to the seaplane tender *Commandant Teste*.

As the sailors evacuated their vessels, demolition crews set the explosives to blow. By 6.45 a.m., fighting had broken out around the *Strasbourg* and *Foch*, which saw the deaths of one French officer and five sailors wounded. The ships' guns had turned on the German tanks and the Axis officers tried to negotiate with Laborde, captain of *Strasbourg*, for the surrender of his vessel. Admiral Laborde simply told the Germans it was too late and that his ship was already sunk. As she settled on the bottom, Laborde ordered the demolition charges be set off, destroying the armament and igniting the fuel stores. Soon after, the cruiser *Colbert* exploded.

The captain of the cruiser *Marseillaise* ordered his ship to be capsized. German troops, who had requested they be allowed aboard, were refused, and the ship sank soon after, before exploding and burning for a week. With explosions going on around, those troops trying to board the *Algérie* tried to persuade her captain that scuttling was forbidden. The request was ignored and the ship would be alight for twenty days as her fuel and anything combustible aboard burned out.

In dry dock was the cruiser *Jean de Vienne*. Her charges were disarmed by the Germans but her open sea cocks flooded her, causing her to sink and block the dry dock. *Dunkerque*'s captain at first refused to scuttle his vessel but eventually she was sunk too, the charges being blown through the holes caused by a British torpedo attack on her previously, with explosives used to destroy her machinery. Nearby was the cruiser *La Galissonnière*, which sank too. One of the ships which the German troops managed to board was the cruiser *Dupleix*. The troops forced the French sailors out of the way and managed to close the seacocks. While this was being undertaken, her captain ordered shortened fuses and the setting off of the charges in her main armament. Soon the ship was ablaze and despite the efforts of the German troops, both French and Germans abandoned ship. With the flames reaching her torpedo stores, the ship was finally sunk as they exploded.

In all, seventy-seven major vessels met their end on 27 November 1942 and Operation Lila could have been deemed to have been a failure. The total of major ships included three battleships, seven cruisers, fifteen destroyers, thirteen torpedo boats and twelve submarines, as well as a training ship and numerous tugs and smaller vessels. The fires burned for three weeks and a pall of smoke remained

Above: German soldiers look on at the *Strasbourg*, which sits on the bottom having sunk some 20 feet into the mud. *Below:* A French destroyer sunk, but with her guns still above the water.

Above: German soldiers resting on the beach at Toulon with the remains of two of the French destroyers in the background.

over Toulon through December. Commander of the Free French Forces, General de Gaulle, criticised the Vichy Admirals for not ordering the fleet to set sail, but many of the larger vessels would have needed time to prepare for sailing, which they did not have on the morning of the 27th. However, four submarines, including the *Casablanca* and *Marsouin*, which both reached Algiers, the *Glorieux*, which berthed at Oran, and the *Iris*, which sailed for Barcelona and internment made it to safety, as did one surface ship, the *Leonor Fresnel*, which reached Algiers too. Another submarine, the *Vénus*, was scuttled in the entrance to the harbour.

Italian teams tried to salvage numerous ships. They salvaged most of the cruisers, with some providing valuable scrap metal for the war effort and two, the *Jean de Vienne* and *La Galissonière* entering Italian naval service as FR11 and FR12. Proper repair of these ships proved impossible due to Allied bombing, and shortages of fuel would have meant their entry into service would have been unlikely if Italy had continued in the war into 1944.

The Germans had seen much of the fleet destroyed as they watched on the quaysides, but they did manage to capture a raggle-taggle bunch of smaller ships. These included three disarmed destoyers, four damaged submarines, three merchant ships and two rather old battleships, the *Condorcet* and the *Océan*, which had been disarmed long before as well as numerous tugs and small vessels.

The battleship *Provence* did provide two turrets, which were removed and used in fortifications to provide cover guarding the port of Toulon. With four 340-mm guns, they were destroyed in 1944 by Allied battleships. The flagship, *Strasbourg*, was raised on 17 July 1943 by Italian sailors, but the armistice of September saw her handed to the Germans. In April 1944, she was handed back to the Vichy French, and sunk again on 18 August 1944. Salvaged once more she was finally scrapped in 1955 after being used for underwater explosive tests. Her sister, *Dunkerque*, scuttled in dry dock, was a total loss; dismantling took place and she was finally removed in 1944. The seaplane carrier *Commandant Teste* was refloated after the war and considered for conversion into an escort carrier. She was instead scrapped in 1950.

While the German High Command considered the attempted capture of the fleet to be a failure, Hitler himself considered it a success, having denied the Allies the fleet, keeping the balance of sea power in the Mediterranean at a status quo and rendering the Vichy French government effectively powerless too. Perhaps, if there had not been over two weeks from the first invasion of Vichy France to the attempts to capture the fleet, the French navy might not have had time to prepare all of the charges and scuttle so many ships. The scuttling also denied parts of the port of Toulon to both Axis and Allied forces as it was not until the late 1940s that all of the ships were cleared, and spilled fuel oil made the harbour dangerous for at least two years after the scuttling. We shall leave the last word to Admiral Darlan, who had told Churchill that the French fleet would never fall into German hands. In early December 1942, Winston Churchill received a letter from Darlan, in which Darlan wrote; 'Prime Minister you said to me "I hope you will never surrender the fleet." I replied, "There is no question of doing so." It seems to me you did not believe my word. The destruction of the fleet at Toulon has just proved that I was right.'

Below: This French submarine escaped from Toulon and is shown arriving at Algiers to fight for the Allies. The only remaining German stronghold in northern Africa by this point was Tunisia.

Top: These Desert Rats of the 8th Army show their obvious delight at reoccupying Tobruk. Severely lacking supplies, especially fuel, Rommel is pushed back and decides to withdraw from El Alamein. *Bottom:* Merchant vessels lie in the harbour at Mersa Matruh, Egypt, and further damage inflicted by Allied aircraft is evident to the jetties and stores. This seaport on the Mediterranean coast had been a vital landing point for the Afrika Korps' supplies.

Top right: This must be one of the most iconic images from the desert war. It shows Australian troops advancing on a strong-point under the cover of a smokescreen.

Middle right: After the Battle of El Alamein, the desert is littered with damaged and abandoned equipment. This British soldier is examining the remains of a German AdKfz2 half-track known as a Kettenkrad. This light gun tractor had a motorcycle-style front wheel for steering, obviously missing on this example.

Bottom right: This column of Italian prisoners, captured during the fighting in El Alamein, is being led by a guard into the 'cage', an open-air holding area formed with barbed wire.

Above: Members of the Afrika Korps 90th light division are being relieved of their equipment after being taken prisoner at El Alamein.

'Now this is not the end. It is not even the beginning of the end, but it is, perhaps, the end of the beginning.'

Winston Churchill*, speaking in November 1942 on the Allied victory at El Alamein.*